"This is the kind of book that could only be the fruit of long, honest, and self-critical experience. Bill Robinson looks at Jesus' style of leadership: that Jesus *dwelt* with those he led, that he was *seen by* (transparent to) those he led, that he *reflected* his Father's glory rather than hugged it to himself, that he spoke with both grace *and* truth. This is a truly Christian discernment of what might be wise action, gleaned always from within earshot of the cries of those in most need of help."

Iain Torrance, President of Princeton Theological Seminary,
Moderator of the Church of Scotland,
Chaplain-in-Ordinary to HM The Queen in Scotland

"I experienced Bill Robinson's inspirational leadership, 'up close and personal,' for about a decade at Whitworth. In this delightful and example-filled book, I learn how he does it: he is a deeply committed and very happy follower of Jesus of Nazareth—in the most remarkable and creative ways. May his kind multiply!"

F. Dale Bruner, Emeritus Professor of Theology, Whitworth University

"Bill Robinson's *Incarnate Leadership* is insightful, practical, and even inspiring. First, I am convinced that Bill has discerned correctly the central leadership priorities Jesus demonstrated in the Bible's Gospels. I love Bill's 'plain talk.' It helps me know that though this book is rooted in biblical truth and is set within well-developed leadership theory, it is also a down-to-earth guide toward how to lead in a way that honors God and genuinely helps people. The book will teach me how to go about my service in that very Jesus-like way."

Greg Waybright, Pastor of the Lake Avenue Church, Pasadena
Former president of Trinity Evangelical Divinity School

"*Incarnate Leadership* is written by one who knows about leadership from a depth of experience. It rings with authenticity as does Bill Robinson himself. Frankly, I have not seen a book that challenges the reader quite like this one. The call to be transparent, real, and even authentic should speak to any who dares to lead."

\ndrew K. Benton, President, Pepperdine University

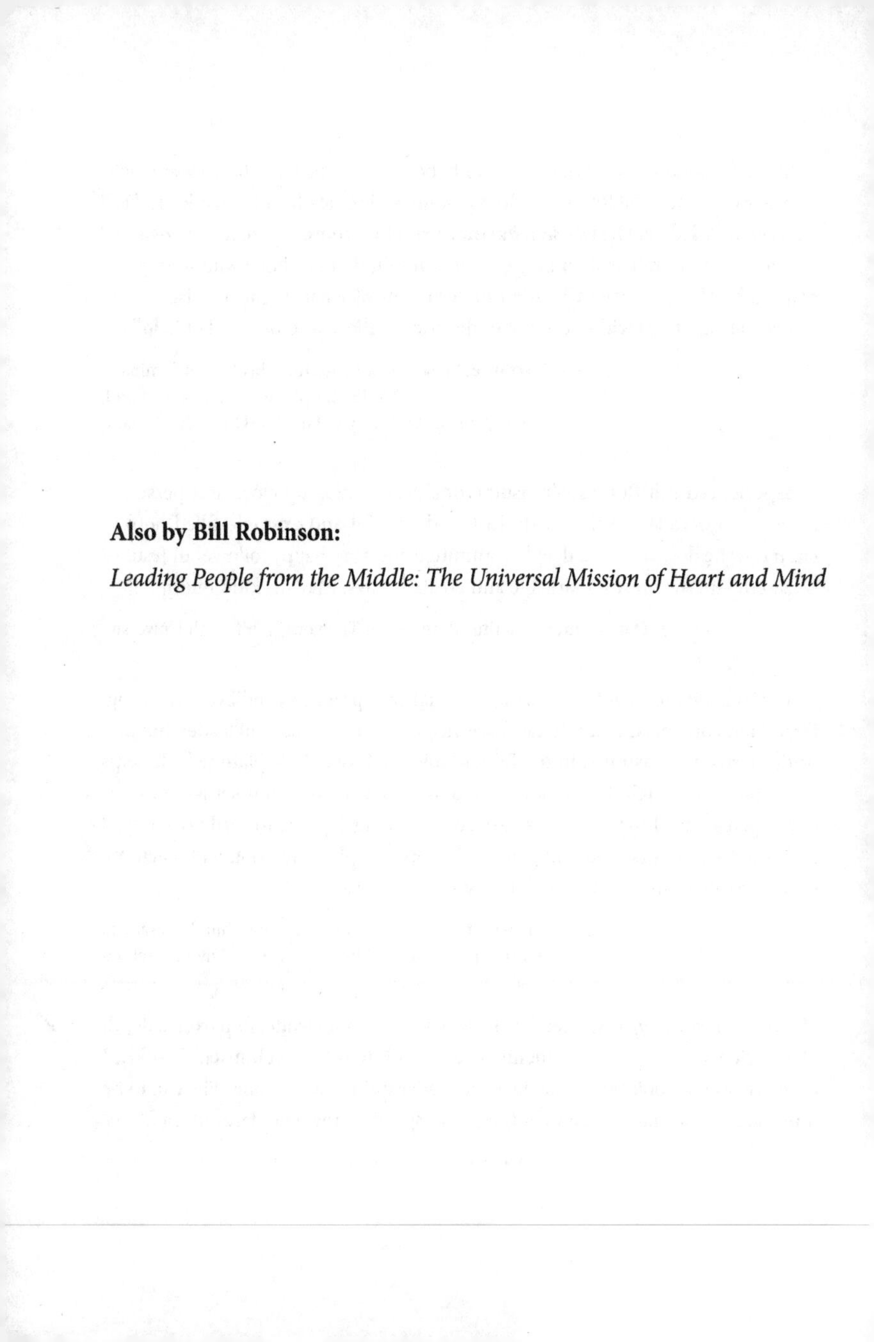

Also by Bill Robinson:

Leading People from the Middle: The Universal Mission of Heart and Mind

INCARNATE LEADERSHIP

5 LEADERSHIP LESSONS
from the LIFE OF JESUS

BILL ROBINSON

ZONDERVAN®

ZONDERVAN

Incarnate Leadership

Requests for information should be addressed to:

Zondervan, *3900 Sparks Dr. SE, Grand Rapids, Michigan 49546*

This edition: 978-0-310-53087-9 (softcover)

Library of Congress Cataloging-in-Publication Data

Robinson, Bill
Incarnate leadership : five leadership lessons from the life of Jesus / Bill Robinson.
p. cm.
Includes bibliographical references and index [if applicable].
ISBN 978-0-310-29113-8 (hardcover, printed)
1. Leadership—Religious aspects—Christianity. 2. Jesus Christ—Leadership. I. Title.
BV4597.53.L43R65 2009
253—dc22 2008028052

Interior design: Ben Fetterley

Printed in the United States of America

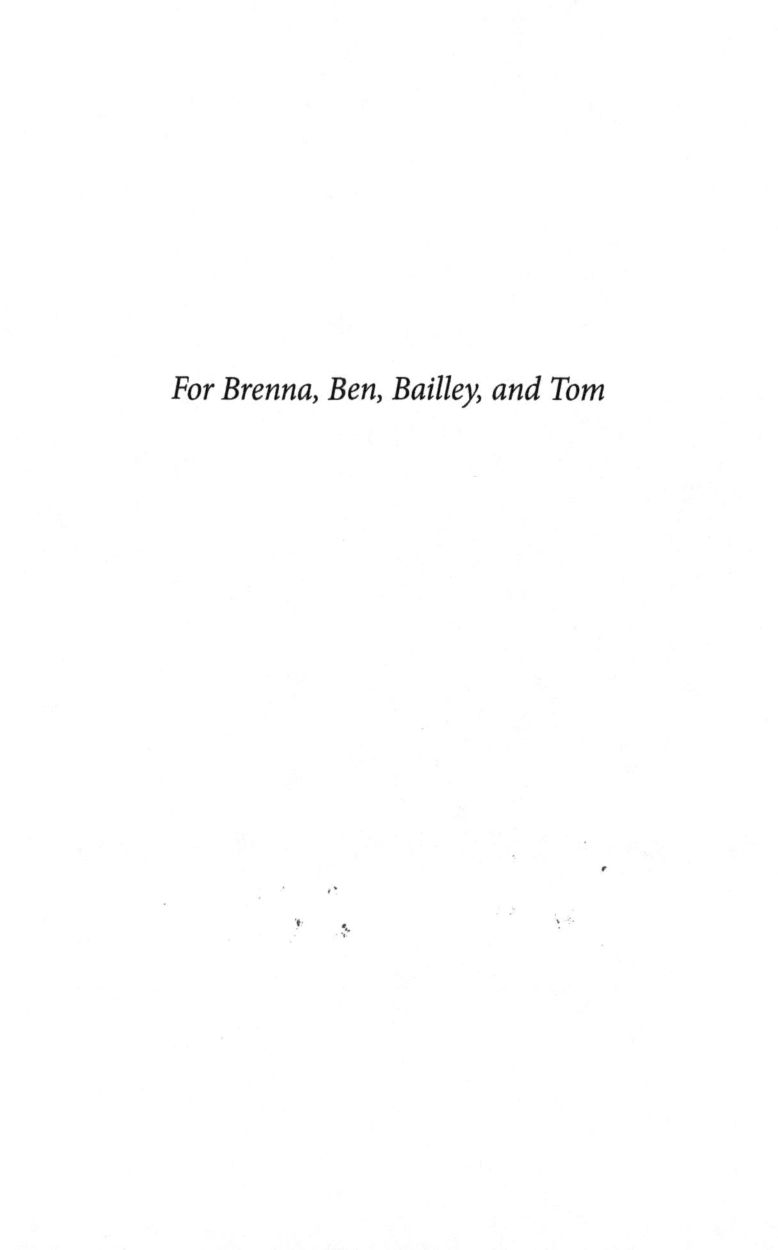

For Brenna, Ben, Bailley, and Tom

Contents

Foreword

We both entered pastoral ministry at about the same time in our lives, but thirty years apart. Both of us had parents who were also pastors, so we've been thoroughly baptized (through immersion, not sprinkling!) in congregational leadership for many years. We've seen the trends come and go, the fads rise and fall. And we've noticed the accompanying vocabulary which has reflected these changes and developments. What we've noticed is lacking in most leadership lexicons is the distinct language and values of the Scriptures.

Far too often the church has adopted the language, the values, and strategies of the marketplace to articulate its unique mission. But the kingdom of God is not a business enterprise, and the *missio dei* is unlike any business plan ever formulated. God's *means* cannot be disconnected from God's *ways.* And God's way has always been intensely personal. Faith-based leadership, therefore, is not as much about what we do as who we are. The miracle of the incarnation demonstrated long ago to our world that God takes us seriously and God relates to us personally, not with mere words, but with incarnated words—true humanity, words that become flesh. God became one of us and lived among us in order to lead us out of darkness and into a marvelous light. Remarkably enough, God's chosen way for leading us to salvation and liberation—through the humanity of Jesus—remains his preferred way: incarnating divinity through humanity to love a hurting, sinful world. But leadership fails—every time—when it becomes mechanistic, formulaic, or in any way impersonal or relationally anemic. The French talk of *deformation professionelle* — a liability, a tendency to defect, that is inherent in the role one has assumed as, say, a physician, a lawyer, a priest. If there is *deformation* to which leadership in the church (and in Christian ministry) is liable it is depersonalization: taking a position on a pedestal and treating the people down below as projects or causes or problems.

In our conversations together over the years reflecting on the nature of leadership (mostly pastoral work, in our cases), we agreed early on that leading a church in the '60s, '70s, and '80s (Eugene) was a very different experience than leading one in the '90s and beyond (Eric). A year or two into the organization of a new church, Eric called Eugene on the phone for some advice related to a developmental issue he was attending to. "Dad, what did you do when you got to this point? I'm stuck." A long pause. And then this reply: "You know, I never had to deal with that in my congregation. This is a very different world you're working in. I guess you'll just have to figure it out."

The world is changing more rapidly than anyone even knows and everyone in a position of leadership struggles to keep up in order to make the necessary adaptations along the way. We "figure it out" as we go, learning from our mistakes, engaging in experiments, taking risks, borrowing ideas from others. These are exciting, challenging times for leaders, at least for those who are willing to figure it out along the way.

The pages which follow invite us to step off the bandwagon piled high with the latest leadership trends and recover the ever-ancient, ever-fresh wisdom of incarnational leadership, and not as just another paradigm to try on for size, but as God's chosen way. In this book, our friend Bill Robinson points to Jesus, not as a mere model for us to emulate, but as the one who incarnates his very presence through us. What God did in Christ, God does through us as well.

Deeply personal and refreshingly honest, this book emerges, not so much from research or scholarly objectivity (although there is plenty of that too) as it does from the lively interaction with students, staff, and faculty which has come to define Bill's leadership style, the style that sets him apart as an incarnate leader himself: not merely personable, but thoroughly personal.

We have watched him live out what he has written here, watched the words become flesh and dwell among us. He has practiced the inversion of biblical leadership: "If any of you want to be great, you must be the servant of all." He has managed to avoid the seductive, "antigravitational" pulls to the distant top, remaining instead engaged in his community and with the people he's been called to love and serve. Before students show up for freshman orientation Bill has already prayed for them. Chances are very good that he already knows their name. He is as comfortable taking off his shirt and playing a pickup game of basketball as he is putting on his academic gown and conferring diplomas to his students. Either way, and including everything in between, he leads from *among* his campus-congregation, thereby incarnating the presence of the risen Lord who shows us how to do it.

Bill has been a leadership mentor to many people, through his writing and through his relationships. His effectiveness as both a leader and mentor, however, is possible only because he has been a serious, disciplined apprentice under the lordship and the leadership of Jesus Christ, "who, though he was in the form of God did not count equality with God as something to be grasped, but humbled himself, taking the form of a servant."

In a world saturated with books on leadership most of us are (rightly) skeptical about yet another one. Yet, if by some special dispensation of grace you don't already have leadership books in your personal library, and you genuinely desire to be a distinctively and unimpressive *Christian* leader, this is the only one — and likely the last — you'll ever need.

Eric E. Peterson, *Colbert, Washington*

Eugene H. Peterson, *Lakeside, Montana*

Acknowledgments

I wish to thank my friends who read the first draft and gave very influential direction: Jack Burns, Dale Soden, Kathy Storm, Jon Lewis, and Aaron McMurray.

I am also indebted to Lyn Cryderman and Ryan Pazdur for their excellent editorial work, and to Sylvia Hedrick for all kinds of help. Thanks especially to Lyn for creating the chapter sidebars and discussion and reflection questions.

Props to Shakey, Chuck, Alan, Lar, Dave, Pat, Steve, Boyd, Ron, and Ken, although I'm not sure what for. Thanks to Andy and Nathan for their example, and to Alan, Emily, Mike, and Caterina for their tolerance. And acknowledgments to my many dear friends and family members upon whom I rely so heavily. In every way, I am sustained by these relationships.

My deepest gratitude goes to the Whitworth University community in general, and to my dear friends on the president's cabinet in particular, for making me a better leader than I was ever meant to be.

And the biggest and best thanks goes to Bonnie Robinson, my favorite and best leader.

Never Stop Learning from Him

On Monday morning, February 4, 2008, every sports page in the world heralded the New York Giants' astonishing Super Bowl upset over the undefeated New England Patriots. And the big story within the story? Giants' head coach Tom Coughlin pulled off the shocker with ... nice. Entering the season with his boss grumbling, "He's our coach this year; we'll see what happens after that," Coughlin decided he needed a leadership makeover. Jackie McMullen of the *Boston Globe* reported an incident that took place on media day, seventy-two hours before the big game:

> A boy no more than eight or nine years old was handed a microphone ... and he made a beeline toward Giants' coach Tom Coughlin, who spotting the junior inquisitor leaned over in an almost grandfatherly fashion and tenderly attended to his question. "I hear you've been a lot nicer this year," said the child. "Who put you up to that?" said the coach to gales of laughter.
>
> After going 8 – 8 in the 2007 season, Tom Coughlin met with his veteran players. They told him he yelled too much, communicated too little, and listened barely at all. Veteran player Michael Strahan calls the change, "a transformation, sometimes I barely recognize him." (*Boston Globe*, January 30, 2008)

Tom Coughlin spent three years trying to change his players. It didn't work. So he decided to change himself. And that's what changed his players. Now they're all sporting Super Bowl rings.

Whenever a student of leadership hears a story like Coughlin's, a predictable line of questioning is not far behind: *Can leaders really change? How embedded is my leadership style? Should I shoot for transformation or settle for tweaking? Are leaders born or made? Is it nature or nurture that makes a leader?*

The answer to the nature-nurture question gives us hope for change. *Both* nature and nurture shape the way people lead. Social scientists and parents with more than one child agree: DNA is a pretty potent influence on the way people behave. And I don't think we can change the water in our gene pool. We have to lead with *our* gifts and *our* calling. When King Saul offered David some fancy armor to fight Goliath, David declined. He played to his strength. He stuck with his slingshot. He must have spent a lot of time developing his technique. I doubt if he was just born a good shot.

And so it is with good leaders. They don't waste time longing for different armor. They develop the gifts God gave them. They hone and improve those gifts. They never stop learning how to use their gifts more effectively. And they change. They get better. And they get nervous at the first sign of stagnation.

My own leadership gifts seemed to unfold as I grew up. As a youth, I led recklessly, usually in the wrong direction. But I've gotten better, both in how and where I lead. I am still learning new ways to grow my gifts and use them more wisely. Anyone who claims to have learned all of life's big lessons in kindergarten didn't go to my kindergarten.

We are influenced by nature *and* nurture, but we are imprisoned by neither.

Yes, we are influenced by nature *and* nurture, but we are imprisoned by neither. We can all become better leaders if we work at it. And one of the ways we work at it is by paying attention to the way great leaders lead. That's what this book is about — paying attention to a great leader.

Like most baby boomers, I witnessed the difference between authority and leadership. My generation was suspicious of those in authority. Our heroes were not the big position holders. We saw our leaders emerge from streets and campuses, churches and neighborhoods. Many of them were angry. They cried out against the war in Vietnam and racial injustice. My anger was diluted with wistfulness. The plight of my classmates in Vietnam made me long for peace. The anguish of my friends who suffered racial and gender discrimination made me long for equality. And my often wobbly but durable belief that ultimate peace could be found only in Jesus Christ made me long for "thy kingdom come."

For the most part, I watched from the sidelines. I really did want things to change, but I just didn't know what to do. I felt helpless. Now, I can see how those years affected the way I lead today. My leadership bears the mark of one who stood as an eyewitness to authorities and conventions that were flat-out wrong. What I was taught to hold sacred ... was not.

When I left college, I did not have "leader" in my career goals. Like many of my generation, I really didn't have much of a plan. We were one of the first generations programmed to see education as a necessary step toward a brighter future. We thought of going to college like getting a car. Even if you didn't know where you were going, it would help you get around. I probably had some ideas about what I wanted to do with my life, but they weren't grand enough that I can remember them now.

Today, I am responsible for leading a small university—a job that I have been doing since I was thirty-six years old. I'm a little sketchy on how I got from being an aimless college student to a college president. Maybe because there weren't too many baby boomers running colleges and businesses, I started this job with a different understanding of leadership than most people in power. Even today, I'm considered a leadership oddball by many of my peers. I guess I'm proud of that. I have no desire to be a typical college president. Plus, I'm a Whitworth *Pirate,* and buccaneers are known for their daring. I'm pretty sure you don't have to be a Pirate to lead, but it is hard to lead without courage. It's especially hard if we want our leadership to be influenced by the example of Jesus. And that's *specifically* what this book is about — following Christ's example to make us better leaders.

What this book is *not* about is bashing Christian leaders. Frankly, I do not find the gaping "leadership vacuum" that has observers of the church and other ministries wringing their hands. I have witnessed excellent leadership from talented and trained leaders who are building strong churches, ministries, and businesses. I salute them and I learn from them. I have neither the right nor the desire to lob uninformed criticism grenades that rain down shrapnel on all Christian leaders. But I cannot believe how many Christian leaders feel besieged. In the last three days, I have spoken with two very successful, very stressed-out pastors. Both have been in their churches for more than a decade. Both have seen growth flatten and criticism rise. Both can name countless other tall-steeple pastors also ducking fire. I'm reminded of the often painted Saint Sebastian — his countenance filled with despair, and his torso filled with darts.

I would never suggest that good leadership keeps everybody happy. But I wonder how our people would respond if we took more leadership lessons from Christ. I fear that those of us who lead Christian organizations have drawn more from the texts of *Harvard Business Review* than from the leadership texts of Christ's life. I think we have done a better job of making Christ the center of our faith than the center of our leadership.

We want to lead well, to lead as Christ led. So we read the best stuff we can get on leadership, and there are some great resources from the secular world. Almost thirty years ago I had lunch with Bill Hybels, pastor of the gargantuan Willow Creek Church in Barrington, Illinois, which at that time was a small church meeting in a theater. Even then, I remember Bill making reference to lessons church leaders could learn from leadership guru Peter Drucker. Bill learned the lessons well. Today, the writings of Jim Collins, Tom Peters, and Malcolm Gladwell occupy space on pastors' shelves next to commentaries and reference books. And that's great. I believe the church recognizes the critical importance of good leadership.

But maybe we've gotten too fixated on leadership per se. Perhaps our desire to be good leaders has elbowed its way in front of our desire to be imitators of Christ. That thought began to take shape for me on December 24, 2000, as I sat in a Christmas Eve service thinking about everything except baby Jesus. For some reason, the familiar words of John 1:14—*And the Word became flesh, and dwelt among us; and we beheld his glory, the glory of the only begotten of the Father, full of grace and truth*—seized me in a new way that night. What I heard was not a Bible verse, but the voice of a faithful follower introducing his leader to the world.

Perhaps our desire to be good leaders has elbowed its way in front of our desire to be imitators of Christ.

At the time I was on my first sabbatical after fourteen years as a college president, and I had just spent a week in seclusion writing the last two chapters for a book that traced the history of leadership theory in the twentieth century. It had been interesting reviewing all the leadership literature I had studied as a doctoral student—back when I "knew everything" and had even thought about becoming a leadership consultant. (Of course, then I got a job and actually had to provide leadership, after which it took me little time to turn in my "expert" badge.) Because the book was intended primarily for a secular audience, I did not explicitly present a Christian perspective on leadership.

And then came my Christmas Eve jolt. When the minister read the famous advent verse, "And the Word became flesh ...," I heard a stunning description of leadership. I didn't know whether to feel gleeful or depressed. I had just written a whole book on this subject; I was *so* done. But the gospel writer John teamed up with the Holy Spirit of God to reveal one verse that offered more wisdom than I could find in all of my book's 256 pages. Since that night, I haven't stopped asking myself five questions that I took from John's introduction of Jesus:

- Jesus dwelt with those he led: *Am I staying close enough to those I lead?*
- Jesus' disciples beheld him: *Am I being transparent with those I lead?*
- The glory of Jesus was a reflection of his Father: *Are my actions reflecting our mission or gathering personal glory?*
- Jesus led with grace and truth: *Am I leading with grace and truth?*
- From the manger to the cross, Jesus sacrificed: *What am I sacrificing for those I lead?*

This book records my understanding and efforts of trying to live into these questions, with an invitation for you to join me. I do not intend to *describe* how Jesus led; others have done that well. Rather, I invite you to think with me about some of the tough, paradoxical challenges in leading with a different kind of authority than one that comes from your title, your office, your salary, or your degrees. How can you not study Jesus if you're looking for that kind of leadership? With no venture capital, no budget, and no formal organization, he changed the world; and two thousand years later he's still changing it.

One Christmas Eve I asked myself the question: what did follower John think about his leader? When he stepped up to the podium to introduce his leader to the world, what did he say? How did he introduce him? In this book I have done my best to report how I have heard and tried to apply John's grand and glorious description of Jesus Christ: *And the Word became flesh, and dwelt among us; and we beheld his glory, the glory of the only begotten of the Father, full of grace and truth.*

I know beyond any doubt that the principles found in John 1:14 have made me a better leader. I hope John's words and Jesus' example lead you as you lead others.

1

Minding the Gap

The Word became flesh and made his dwelling among us. We have seen his glory, the glory of the One and Only who came from the Father, full of grace and truth.

John 1:14

"Mind the gap, please."

If you've ever traveled on the London Underground, you're familiar with those words. Ignore them, and you can fall headlong into the space between the platform and train. As leaders, we face a different sort of gap — the gap between the positions we occupy and the needs of those we lead. Some of us ignore the gap. Others of us stumble trying to cross the gap. But in Jesus we find a leader who stepped across the gap. His incarnation bridged the unfathomable chasm between God and sinful humanity. It's no wonder that as we look at the way Jesus led, we see a leader who was never too distant from his followers.

I've heard a lot of Christian leaders describe their leadership style as *incarnational*. You've got to admire their nerve. I think I know what they mean, but it's hard not to picture them snapping their suspenders as they respond to the question, "What's your leadership style?"

"Incarnational, of course."

"You mean like God becoming man?"

"Yeah, that's how I lead. I lead like God."

We all do a lot of big talking about how close we are to our people. But are we? As much as we try to mind the gap between our positions and the people we lead, the antigravitational pull upward is powerful. Christian leaders are not exempt from the tug.

SEEING BEYOND OURSELVES

Incarnation. Humility. Access. Other-centeredness. John loved these qualities in Jesus. They are at the core of Christlike leadership. But they do not represent the natural curvature of our fallen human condition. Martin Luther was fond of quoting St. Augustine's description of the human condition as "curved in on ourselves." I'm pretty sure the average leader's inward curvature well exceeds that of the general population. Mine does. I do the kind of work that attracts a lot of attention. People are interested in me. My wife says I am especially interested in me. Ouch. I want to be curved outward. I love the people I have been entrusted to lead, but my needs often blind me to their needs. I forget how good it is to be in the midst of my coworkers.

Those of us in leadership positions should give our positions back to the God who chose to stoop, to the God who chose to dwell with his followers. We should do this not only because it is Christlike but because it empowers those we lead. When my board chair steps out of his busy life simply to be with me, it inspires me because I realize he cares about me, not just my job performance. We are image descendants of a God who valued incarnation above all other redemption strategies. Our spiritual DNA moves us toward the magnetic force of leaders who dwell among us.

Recently, I encountered a faculty member who had just returned with twenty-five students from a life-changing experience in Africa. Somehow I failed to remember to ask about his poignant experience.

I did not, however, fail to remember to talk about my stuff and how I was doing. The grace with which he accepted my apology the next day reminded me that the people we lead are often too kind to tell us which way we are curved. If our focus keeps curving in on ourselves, then even when we are in the presence of those we lead, we will not really know them.

We need to ask ourselves the questions that curve toward our people. How much time do we spend with them? Are we eager to be in their presence? Do we make warm inquiries about their lives? What does our "me-them" conversational balance sheet look like? What opportunities are we missing simply to be in the presence of those whom we hope will have confidence in our leadership? I fear too often we fail to look very far beyond ourselves and our to-do lists.

RESISTING THE PEDESTAL

Like many ministry leaders, I am in a line of work that encourages "being above" more than "being with." When I became a college president in 1986, I went to a conference for new presidents. The leadership guru at the event explained how excessive democratization in higher education had rendered presidential authority impotent. He then urged us to stand tall on the pedestal of our position and stave off the efforts of all who would remove us. Interesting advice. I start a job where I have the highest salary, a free car, a free house, the biggest office, a sizeable travel and entertainment budget, and our employees' respect for the office I hold. And my instructions for leading? Climb on a pedestal; create more distance from those I'm supposed to lead. In other words, I should grab more of what I already have at the expense of the one thing I don't have — authentic peer-to-peer relationships.

I didn't take the pedestal advice. I wish I could say my desire to be Christlike kept my feet on the ground, but my reasons for avoiding the pedestal were more social than spiritual. I just love college students and

I admired our faculty and staff. I didn't feel my role should exempt me from their friendship. I'm sure most pastors and most of us in ministry enter our positions with a deep desire to befriend our congregations and our staffs. But somehow we feel the need to maintain distance. Our people elevate us. We let them do it. And then one day we hear we're out of touch. We begin to wonder if we got put on the pedestal to make us easier targets.

I've come to the conclusion that people try to park us in high places because they think that's where we belong. It's a way of expressing respect. But that's not what they really want. I'm still waiting for a student or staff person to criticize me for being insufficiently aloof. People love to see leaders on their turf. John was no exception. The introduction to his gospel account speaks volumes. If he were doing a newspaper story on Jesus, he would likely open it with the biggest, most ostentatious miracle he could find. Maybe that's what he did. Maybe to John, Jesus' biggest miracle was the first one he saw: God walking around in Galilee. Immanuel. God with us. Astonishing! Miraculous! The best thing imaginable.

People try to park us in high places because they think that's where we belong. It's a way of expressing respect. But that's not what they really want.

Not long ago I talked my wife into renting the movie *Lawrence of Arabia*. (I didn't tell her this epic took an epoch to watch.) My favorite scene in this entire, interminable film is the point at which the Bedouin ruler fully accepts the leadership of an interloping British soldier, T. E. Lawrence. After Lawrence removes his British uniform, wet from an act of heroism, the *sharif* throws it into the fire and presents Lawrence with full Arab regalia. Through this act, the Bedouin ruler ushered Lawrence across the divide of race, culture, and colonialism. Lawrence took on the likeness of the Bedouins he sought to lead—he became Lawrence *of Arabia*. At a very primal level, we hear incarnation echoing from our *imago deo* as the ultimate means of reducing the gap. Ironically, we want to follow our leaders when they come alongside of us more than when they are out in front of us.

THE CHOICE TO DWELL AMONG

But "crossing over" doesn't just happen. We have to make a deliberate choice. We have to be intentional in resisting the forces that create gaps between ourselves and those we have been called to lead. As I began my career in higher education, a colleague's sudden departure made me a good choice (actually, the only choice) to fill his leadership role. I did pretty well in the role, so it wasn't too long before I got bumped again. I was, as they say, moving up. There is nothing unhealthy or insidious about this. You are given an assignment, you do your best, and you get promoted. So far, so good. Except the higher you go, the harder it is to stay connected with those you have been called to lead. At first, this troubles you, but you are comforted by a new set of peers at your elevated level who help you accept the inevitability of distance. Then at some point — who can say exactly when — you lose touch. *This* is insidious.

For some leaders the upward drift is quiet and incremental. I spoke recently at a retreat for business and church leaders from Houston, home to the former Enron Corporation. To a person, those who knew Ken Lay, the late, shamed Enron CEO, considered him a fine human being who allowed himself to get insulated high above his people. He ended up with a gap he never would have imagined, but ultimately it did him in.

Some leaders get stuck on the pedestal by the glue of their own egos. They listen to their sycophants. (King Darius ended up tossing Daniel in the lions' den when he got suckered into making himself a god.) I'm not suggesting that we relinquish all the perks and privileges that come with leadership. But I do feel our best bet for being Christlike leaders is to bridge the gap, evacuate every pedestal. Would Jesus have a special parking space, a plexiglass pulpit, a cavernous office? Would he refer to himself as "Jesus S.O.G" as readily as we call ourselves "Rev. Dr. Jones"? Those of us in leadership need to ask ourselves a few pedestal questions:

- What are the pedestals or positions in my life and work that distance me from those I have been called to lead?
- When are the times that being in the midst of my coworkers comes most naturally?
- How can I use my leadership position to get closer to my people?
- What pulls me above or away from those I lead?
- Who can help me narrow the gap?

WORKING OURSELVES DOWN

Recently I was reading F. Dale Bruner's masterpiece commentary on Matthew (*Matthew, a Commentary: The Christbook, Matthew 1–12* [Erdmans, 2004]). I'm not sure which of my demons had been teasing me, but for some reason I was studying the temptations of Christ in Matthew 4, so I decided to check out what Professor Bruner had to say about that wilderness battle. As usual, he made a fascinating observation. In each of the three temptations, Satan leads Jesus to higher ground. They go from the "wilderness" up to the "top of the temple," and then up again to a "very high mountain." Satan knows the intoxicating air of exaltation deepens our thirst for the pride of life. The Spirit, on the other hand, is more of a down-and-outer. The Spirit led Jesus *down* to the Jordan, *down* into its muddy baptismal waters, and *out* to the wilderness to be tempted. This is scary stuff. Satan points us up. God points us down. And what we discover is that what culture deems low, God considers high.

Sometimes we're surprised to find out the people we lead are more impressed by down than up. Two weeks ago I got an email from an alumnus:

Hey Bill,

I was just talking to my friend who was ragging about how her college president drives a massive SUV and her professors drive gaudy convertibles and I was recalling how you would bike to campus every day.

Whether it was for simplicity or environmentalism, or just convenience, I really appreciate now the message you chose to NOT send to me and other students by not driving the latest and sexiest sports car. I am really growing in my understanding of God as the creator/re-creator as well as [in] my understanding of what it means to be a godly and compassionate world citizen, and it is a huge joy to see examples in people for how to creatively pursue that.

As recorded in Matthew, Jesus book-ends his public ministry with a counterintuitive message. In the Sermon on the Mount (Matthew 5–7) he begins his lessons with the announcement that the scorecard is backwards. Last place is really first place. Then he wraps up his teaching in Matthew 25 by identifying himself with the poor and the hungry and the imprisoned. These passages can be haunting as we scramble up to the top. Leading like Christ requires us to find the holy ground of down and out. When we see it, we almost don't recognize it.

Leading like Christ requires us to find the holy ground of down and out.

After fortifying my resolve with Bruner's treatment of the temptations, I decided to skip all the guilt and shame I can count on when the Sermon on the Mount reminds me that many of my values are upside down. So I hurdled Matthew 5–7 and went straight to chapter 8. The opening words delivered a metaphor I had never noticed — words of incarnation, words of leadership. Matthew 8:1 says, "When he came down from the mountainside, large crowds followed him."

The leaders we love to follow don't get too comfortable on the mountain. When they're out of touch, they can feel it; and they don't like it. But many leaders get seduced by *up*. They lie to themselves — or they believe somebody else's lies — that distance breeds respect. So they hover. They guard the gap rather than narrow it. They become accustomed to the mountain, and the strong sense of privilege with which they enter their positions gets replaced by a stronger sense of enjoyment and entitlement.

All industries foster implicit and explicit forces that separate leaders from their people, though few with the shamelessness of higher education and the church. We always have a good excuse for staying on the mountain. But the crowds followed Jesus *when he came down*.

PLUNGING INTO THE MIDDLE

After Jesus comes down from the mountain he wastes no time getting himself into the middle of things. A leper kneels before Jesus and asks to be healed. Now, we know from the next miracle in this passage (the healing of the centurion's paralyzed servant back home) that Jesus can do long-distance healing, so who could have blamed him for lobbing a miracle across the unclean zone? Further, lepers need their space. Not even Jesus should violate that. But the first act of the Great Physician came as he "reached out his hand and touched the man" (Matthew 8:3). He broke the rules. He healed the broken.

Asking the wrist bracelet question, "What would Jesus do?" can be unsettling. In this case, we know what Jesus did. The really unsettling question is "What would Bill do?" How do I respond to the unlovely person who needs me? I cannot read of Jesus healing the leper without thinking about one person who really can lay claim to incarnational leadership. In 1873 a strong, healthy thirty-three-year-old Belgian priest went to Molokai, Hawai'i with a longing to minister to a colony of lepers. Damien de Veuster heard God's call to the *least of these*. With astounding energy and effectiveness, he went about improving the conditions of these hopeless outcasts. Father Damien did everything he could do ... everything except reach out his hand and touch them. Choosing to do that, he was told, meant choosing to become one of them. But ultimately, that is the choice he made. He plunged headfirst into a physical, moral, and spiritual cesspool. A slow, wasting disease that would lead to an early and disfigured death was his certain sentence. And the sentence was not commuted. He died at age forty-nine.

Father Damien built buildings, improved health conditions, attracted funding, and raised awareness for this colony of outcasts. But the single greatest act credited with burning the gospel of Christ into the hearts of his people came when Father Damien gathered together the whole colony, stood up to speak, and said, "We lepers ...."

With Jesus, Father Damien literally took on the likeness of sinful flesh. He neither died on the cross nor redeemed the lepers' souls, but he heard God's call to sacrifice. To him, he could not be among his people without suffering with his people.

All of us should ask what it means and what it does not mean to stand with those we lead. When Christ became a man, he did not cease to be God. And when we come alongside those we lead, we do not relinquish the roles and responsibilities of our positions. To do so would be wrong and ineffective. Bridging a gap forcibly or inauthentically ends up creating a toll bridge with little traffic. If I think coming down from the mountain to be with our students means getting a nose ring and sagging my pants halfway down my butt, I'm an idiot. Not only will I tire of the charade, but when the game is over the students are left with a different person than the one they followed—and that's costly to the leader and followers alike.

If I think coming down from the mountain to be with our students means getting a nose ring and sagging my pants halfway down my butt, I'm an idiot.

For me bridging the gap means de-emphasizing the symbols of my position and simply taking the countless opportunities to engage our students, faculty, and staff. My nine colleagues on the president's cabinet are my friends. As friends, we care for each other. We disagree with each other,

THE GAP TEST

Answer yes or no to each question and check your score below:

1. I know the names of every person on my church's or organization's payroll.
2. I eat lunch more often with the people I lead than with the people I'm trying to schmooze.
3. I regularly spend time with my direct reports either in social settings or other events outside my ministry or organization.
4. I instruct my assistant to make every effort to accept appointments with all staff members and constituents in my organization.
5. I do not have a special reserved parking spot.
6. I encourage my subordinates to call me by my first name or some other informal greeting in day-to-day situations rather than use titles such as Doctor or Reverend.
7. When I meet individuals in my office, I do not remain behind my desk or position myself in a way that emphasizes my authority.
8. When I delegate a responsibility to a colleague, I make it clear that I am also delegating the authority to carry out that responsibility.
9. At least once in the last twelve months I have apologized to a colleague.
10. I submit at least annually to a confidential evaluation from my subordinates.

ANSWER KEY:

9–10 yes answers: no gap

7–8 yes answers: mind the gap (NOTE: The author confessed he scored in this range.)

Fewer than 7 yes answers: how's the pedestal?

though we resist personalizing differences or criticisms. Friends trade caution for openness. I don't stop being their president when I'm being their friend, but I don't stop being their friend when I'm being their president, even when things get hard. In fact, one measure of leader-colleague relationships is what happens when things do get hard.

A few years ago in a cabinet meeting, a couple members just pounded me for the way I was handling an issue. They couldn't decide whether I was weak, naïve, or both, but they made it pretty clear that they were not impressed with my performance as a leader. After the meeting I was expecting either an apology or more pounding, neither of which I wanted. But instead my critics gave me a very encouraging message. They thanked me for the open culture, a culture that gave permission to honesty.

Plunging into the middle does not mean leprosy, but it does mean putting ourselves in a position where we can reach out and touch those we lead.

LOVING THOSE WE LEAD

I think it is in God's design that those entrusted to lead others must first love the people they are called to lead. The incarnation of Christ was based on "God so loved . . . ." It is hard for me to imagine living with the stresses that accompany my job if I didn't love our students and staff. Several years ago a parent approached me after I had given the commencement "charge" to our graduating seniors (as if we hadn't charged them enough already!). He said, "It's so easy for you to tell these graduates you have loved them, but I think you do. Thank you." I could not have been more gratified. When pastors, ministry leaders, or any other people in leadership find the gap between themselves and their people widening, it is worth asking if the problem is really the demands of the job or if it's the cooling of their hearts. If we do not love those whom we have been called to lead, then we are not going to be very anxious to come down from the mountain.

The first person I ever saw lead from among his people is still my best example of what it means to love the people you lead. I was twenty-two years old when I met John Thatcher, at that time the owner and president of the company his late father started, Yes Banana Supply, Inc., in Miami, Florida. I worked at John's church, having compromised my commitment to spend a year as a hobo in a warm climate after graduating in January from a college in the U.S. tundra region. John was a man of towering integrity, exactly twice my age. When I would stop by his office to say hello he'd deliver a ritual homily on the physical, moral, social, and spiritual benefits of the banana. My, how he believed in his product! But it wasn't his banana worship that captivated me. It was the walks. On those lucky days when he didn't have bananas in his office, we would head for the yard. Those walks imprinted me forever with a picture of a leader who got from his people what he gave to his people — love and respect. When this man — born of privilege and stationed, almost without choice, in his father's vineyard — walked back among his loaders and truck drivers, it felt like a ticker-tape parade.

I could never keep myself from commenting to John about how his people all seemed so purposeful in their work. Big smiles would cross their faces as they waved, shouting, "Hey, Mr. Thatcher," while darting wherever. John would always attribute their energy and dispositions to his having hired good people. As I got to know John, I discovered it was far more than that. One Sunday after church, John invited me to play golf at his country club. Having never golfed at a country club, I was slack jawed at its opulence from the moment we arrived. So, of course, I asked John how often he golfed at this luxurious course. "Sunday afternoons, that's it," he said ruefully. When I asked why he didn't play more often, he shrugged and said, "I don't think I should be playing golf when my people are working. And, honestly, I'd rather be there with them."

People sense when they are loved by their leaders, when their leaders are drawn to them and desire to be among them. Jesus loved his disciples. He dwelt with them. Familiarity seemed to breed love, not contempt, between Jesus and his followers.

What can we do when our hearts begin to cool, when those we lead annoy us rather than lift us? I think we have to move *toward* the problem. We need to spend more time with our people. For me, several activities have been helpful when I start losing the pull toward those I serve:

- Leaving early for a meeting with the intention of people interruptions occurring en route
- Walking inside of a building rather than past a building (the first time I did this was to get out of the cold; I was warmed in more ways than one)
- Scheduling visits to departments (currently, I'm flunking this one)
- Leaving my office during traffic hours (for students, it's in between classes; for staff it's arrival and departure times)
- Going to our coffee shop, just to mingle
- Asking my work group (president's cabinet) to schedule me into their meetings from time to time
- Telling our student leaders I am anxious to host or cohost student events (last night our IM coordinator arranged a quick dinner in the dining commons for me and one of the intramural teams)

Every one of these activities renews my affection for this community. Being with our people provides both therapy and diagnosis for our hearts. When we dive into the midst of those we lead, it should exhilarate us. If it doesn't, we should resign from our leadership.

FOCUSING ON THE RIGHT PEOPLE

One of my worst life memories is taking our eldest child to the park when she was three years old, only to catch myself acting cool because a couple of moms were also there with their children. Rather than entering into the silliness my precious daughter wanted, I tried to impress two people whom I would never again see and who couldn't have cared less. That is just sick.

My older brother used to wear me out asking the question, "Who are you trying to impress?" I wonder if he ever heard me when I muttered, "Drop dead, Ed." But it's a pretty good question. If I had paid attention, I might have done better at the park. A lot of us leaders try to dazzle people we don't know. I probably impress the guy at the bus stop more than my coworkers or family by driving a hot car (although when we bought a well-used Ford Taurus, our fifteen-year-old son did say it was an embarrassment to our family name).

Dwelling among the people we lead gets us focused on the right people. One of my pastor friends always takes his coffee break with the maintenance staff. He enjoys it, and he understands more than most pastors about their church facilities. A college president friend often travels on team buses and planes to athletic events. The team members love the guy. Another friend who runs a manufacturing operation makes sure he wanders around the shop every day he's in town. We think we don't have enough time for these random acts of engagement, and we're wrong. The dividends are huge.

Sometimes focusing on our people requires less than a minute. Last semester one of our departments hosted a symposium on global warming. For some reason, I was one of the speakers. I noticed a freshman sitting alone whom I'd just met and whose name, surprisingly, I recalled. I heard she was having a typical bout of homesickness, but I didn't have a chance to speak with her after the meeting. As I was walking home I remembered seeing her and decided to shoot her a quick email:

> Was that you listening to me pretend I knew something about global warming? I hope you're doing great. If you ever need to get off campus, give me a holler and you can come over and play our piano. Blessings and best wishes!!! BR

The following Sunday I bumped into her at church, after which she replied by email:

> Great seeing you and visiting with you this morning! Your email made my day yesterday! I would really like to stop by sometime. Have a great rest of the weekend.

Not long after receiving her note, I got one from her dad, just saying thanks for caring about his daughter. Sending an email is a tiny act . . . but evidently not to the student. I invested thirty seconds, but those thirty seconds helped get a freshman off to a good start and comforted a father with the knowledge that someone cared about his kid. Focusing on the right people begets focusing on the right people.

Several years ago a college president asked me, "What's the best thing you've ever read on leadership?" My reply spilled out before I had time to think: "Our students. When I'm with them long enough to listen, they tell me how to lead them." When I spend time and identify with those I lead, it keeps me focused on the right people.

THE PARADOX OF LEADING FROM AMONG

How do we exercise leadership from the middle of the pack? How do we know when to lead the group one moment and then to defer to the group the next? How can we, at once, be the player and the coach? How do we know when to be which?

Navigating any leadership paradox requires artistry more than science. I just returned from a president's cabinet retreat. Our group of ten gets away three times a year for twenty-four hours of fellowship and discussion. It's a great chance to take a collective look at big-picture issues. On this retreat one of the discussion topics centered on organizational structure. We batted around typical questions: *If we were to start from scratch, is this what we would build? Do we have the right people in the right places doing the right things? How does our current structure facilitate or impede communication among us?* For the first half of the discussion I mostly listened and asked a few questions. Nothing seemed to take shape, and I wasn't sure where to point us next. After another half hour, it was clear where everyone stood, all the ideas were on the table, and the information value of the discussion had flattened. So I thanked everyone, summarized what I heard, and told them I had learned what I needed to make some decisions. I ended up making modest adjustments rather than the bold changes I had planned. I didn't feel much like a leader, but listening and adjusting, as opposed to just announcing my plans, ended up being what leadership required in that situation.

"Dwelling among" does not mean forfeiting our responsibilities. Rather, it exposes us to perspectives that enable us to fulfill our duties more effectively. When we position ourselves among those we lead we get better information and make better decisions. We also build trust for those lonely, less popular moves we need to make. People hold more confidence in a leader's ability to anticipate the implications of an action if the leader is close to the people affected. As a rule, honesty and trust will rise with proximity.

As a rule, honesty and trust will rise with proximity.

If God incarnate pitched his tent right in the middle of those whom he led — those whom he called his friends — what should we as leaders do? I am convinced that the place from which Christ would have us lead is not above our people, not in front of our people, not under our people, and not by cell phone with our people. The most powerful position of leadership is *beside* those God calls us to lead. Among them. If Jesus emptied himself to take on the form of a bond servant (Philippians 2:5 – 8), shouldn't we empty ourselves of the pretenses and privileges that create distance between us and our people?

Neither the Bible nor good sense supports all efforts to erase hierarchical differences or the boundaries they create. But relentlessly we need to ask what exaggerates the separation from those we lead, and then attack those barriers. Pedestal leadership is defended more enthusiastically by other people on other pedestals than it is by those we lead.

Apparently, something elemental in God's nature prizes incarnation, the ultimate expression of empathy. What else would prompt God to choose such an agonizing strategy for reaching humanity? I love our students, but I don't feel compelled to register for classes, move into the dorm, commit myself to four years of sleep deprivation, and become one of them. But Jesus did. He became a common man who met a most inglorious death. And if we hope to be Christlike leaders, it will mean narrowing the gap between us and those we lead.

Jesus marched to the cross with those on the low road. Fully God, he left his throne and lived among those he came to save. Now, he has returned to the right hand of God the Father. And there we have a high priest who knows what we're going through, a high priest who was tempted at all points (Hebrews 2:18). It feels good to have a leader who knows our challenges.

Questions for Reflection and Discussion

1. Do you think of yourself as a leader? If so, did you make a conscious decision to become a leader or are you more of a leader by default?
2. What are some of the privileges you enjoy as a leader? How would you explain those privileges to the lowest-paid employee in your church or organization?
3. How do you balance the responsibilities of leading your staff with the desire to also be their friend? Do you think it is possible for a leader to have a genuine friendship with someone who reports to him or her?
4. What's the difference between making a good impression and trying to impress others? Describe a personal example of doing each of these.
5. The author talks about how meaningful tiny or random acts of engagement with one's staff can be. Identify three "tiny acts" you will do this week to identify with the people you lead.

2

Leading Openly

Live as children of light (for the fruit of the light consists in all goodness, righteousness and truth) and find out what pleases the Lord. Have nothing to do with the fruitless deeds of darkness, but rather expose them ... everything exposed by the light becomes visible, for it is light that makes everything visible.

Ephesians 5:8b – 11, 13 – 14a

... and we beheld his glory ...

John 1:14 KJV

A friend of mine told me about working for a company that issued a grim budget warning: "We are in a very tough financial position. Please economize wherever possible." Departments had their budgets cut. Stress levels were on the rise. One day this man's boss called a meeting and announced an event that would honor employees for working so hard during this difficult period. Quite innocently, someone asked the question, "Where are we going to get the money to cover the costs?" Folks were shocked at the answer: "Oh, we have a secret slush fund to cover these sorts of things." Silent confusion filled the room. Certainly, there was nothing sinister about having a special fund to honor the employees. But the surprise that such a fund existed, coupled with incessant messages of austerity, produced a scent of betrayal. Had employees been aware of this budget line, they might have questioned it or applauded it. But both would have been better than being shocked by it. It may be cute when we surprise our children, but it's demoralizing when we surprise our employees. Transparency is a better way to do business.

God becoming man stands as the greatest act of self-disclosure in the history of histories. Unimaginable. In the early days, God denied Moses' request for full disclosure on Mount Horeb with some version of "Sorry Moses, if I do that I'll have to kill you" (see Exodus 33:18 – 23). So God's hand covered Moses' eyes and only God's glory was revealed. But for John, God's glory was beheld in a walking, talking, eating, sleeping Jesus.

Jesus must not have felt the disciples could really know God by simply observing the Word made flesh. So he went further. He put his cards on the table, face up, "Everything that I learned from my Father, I have made known to you" (John 15:15b). When John says, "And we beheld his glory ..." he was not referring to a glimpse or a sighting of Jesus. "Beheld" meant up close. The disciples had an open view of an open leader. Being a Christlike leader requires the same kind of "beholdability." It means being transparent. It means taking the initiative to make known what we have learned.

THE DECISION TO LEAD TRANSPARENTLY

I'm not sure there has been a more corrosive leadership practice than secrecy and unnecessary confidentiality. Information empowers. Ignorance disempowers. It is a question of what leaders want for their people.

But aren't there good reasons for keeping information private? Yes, very good reasons. Information holds immense power and should be disclosed wisely. Christ came to reveal, but he was not reckless in his revelation. He used parables. He timed his disclosures. The best leaders are transparent leaders, but at times information needs to be restricted. For instance:

- It is often best to hold back information that would embarrass or damage people. If no moral issues are involved, we should not disclose information that makes an individual look bad in order to make the organization or ourselves look good.
- We should not disclose information we hold in confidence. Such disclosures destroy trust and discourage openness from those we lead.
- We should not disclose hearsay. Openness requires verification and accuracy.
- We should not disclose information that can only be understood in the context of justifiably confidential information.
- We should not disclose legally protected information, even if we think we're safe. We are not above the law.

Perhaps it is because of these legitimate reasons to withhold information that so many of us leaders have excelled at keeping people in the dark. In my first full-time job, I didn't realize the extent to which confidentiality was a part of the leadership culture. But when I joined the team, almost magically the scrolls opened up before me and I gained access to volumes of information. Some of it was highly confidential and should not have been widely distributed. But much of the information available to the brass would have benefited the troops if only they were granted access.

We have plenty of excuses for cloaking information. For example:

- *Our people just wouldn't understand.* Yup, they're pretty dumb. How condescending! It's true, in the face of consistent concealment, people probably wouldn't understand. But regular openness breeds understanding, and it expresses implicitly the leaders' confidence that people can and do understand. Ten years ago we opened up our budgeting process. People are much more understanding of the facts than they were of what they imagined to be the facts.

- *It's not really any of their business.* Not all information concerns everyone, but don't we want the people we lead to own their work and to support the mission? If we do, then we should treat them as partners. Our business *is* their business. Communicating only on a strict "need to know" basis (and I'll decide what you need to know) is insulting.
- *It takes too much time.* Disclosing information builds trust. If you don't need to spend time building trust, lucky you.
- Some of the information looks bad. If it only looks bad, you can explain it. If it *is* bad, fix it.

I'm somewhat of a student of organizational cultures, so when I speak to various groups, it's always interesting for me to find out about their openness climates. In general, I find one of three questions shapes the organization's commitment to transparency:

- Why should we disclose this information?
- Why shouldn't we disclose this information?
- What information can we disclose that will be helpful?

These ascending levels of openness almost always act as indicators of organizational morale, as noted in the chart on page 43.

Leaders enjoy ready access to a resource that can help them build openness as an organizational value. It's not Google, and it's not Peter Drucker, and it certainly isn't me. It is the simple exercise of listening their way through the organization. Before hiring a high-priced consultant to do a communication audit, leaders should have all the stakeholders

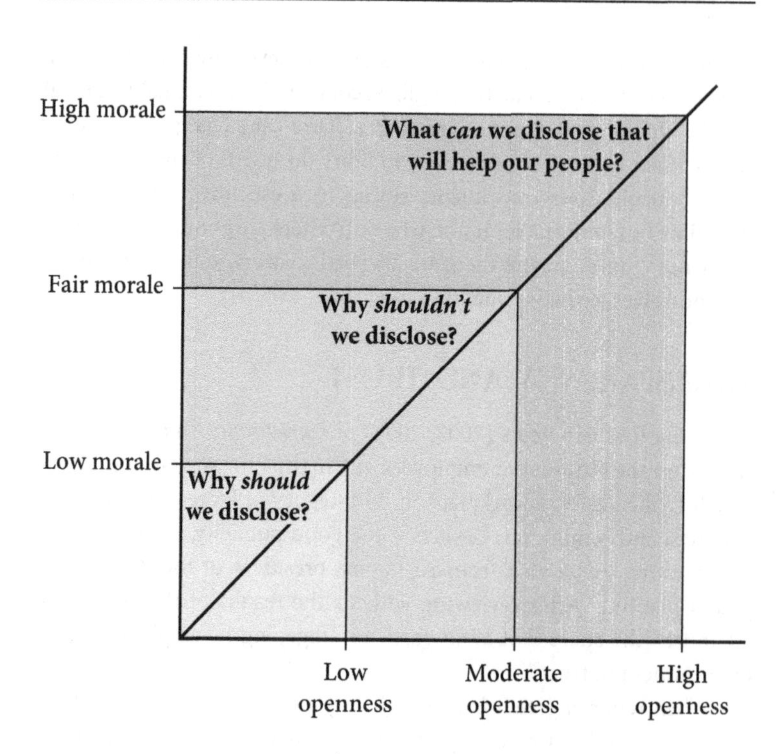

describe what a more open organization would look like to them. Here are some questions to ask your colleagues:

- When were they last surprised by information?
- Would they or could they have done their jobs better with better information?
- What information do they have from which others could benefit?
- When do they think information shouldn't be disclosed?
- What can be disclosed that will position people for greater responsiveness and effectiveness?

In our president's cabinet discussions we never use the phrase, "If people found out." First, they will. Second, we're accountable to our people. Openness invites accountability. If we can't feel good about an action *when* people find out, we shouldn't do it. All of us in ministry should imagine our constituents sitting in a executive staff meeting. Would we be comfortable? If not, why not? There are good answers to the "Why not?" question, but there are also bad answers, and if we're honest with ourselves we know what they are.

TRANSPARENCY AND TRUST

In the first two years (2003, 2004) of *Christianity Today*'s national survey on the attitudes of employees at Christian organizations, Whitworth ranked as best workplace in its category of larger colleges, universities, and seminaries. Besides some good publicity, the reward for that ranking was a visit from Al Lopus, president of the Best Workplaces Institute. After reviewing with us the results of the survey, he attributed the success of Whitworth to "engaging its employees in an environment of trust."

When reporter Helen Lee interviewed me for a follow-up article in *Christianity Today*, I made a pretty big deal out of our commitment to openness and its effect on morale. I mentioned a very open budgeting process, access to expense reports, and the posting of committee minutes as examples of what can contribute to a culture of transparency. I didn't and I still don't claim that we are as transparent as we need to be, but I did identify openness as an indispensable antecedent to trust. A few days later Helen called me back with a question from her editors. "Shouldn't employees have to earn our trust before we place our confidence in them?" I think a better question is, "Shouldn't we have to earn our employees' trust before they put their confidence in us?" We control our behavior, but not our people's. Further, whoever holds the power should bear the responsibility of taking the risk. Trust begets trust, so leaders should make the first move. Transparency offers many benefits, and it's a good first move because it shouts, "I trust you."

Nature abhors a vacuum. So does human nature. We all want to know the *why* behind the *what*. Sometimes we try to figure out *why* even before there is a *what*. When we are feeling an information vacuum, we try to fill it, even if we have to make stuff up. It starts the first time a parent uses the hackneyed "Because I said so!" to explain why you're not allowed to do it, whatever *it* is. My dad used to say that. It made me crazy. I never once said it as a parent because I know what I thought as a kid: "Okay, Dad, I get the authority piece, but you can do better than that. What's to gain by being coy? Clue me in, because if you don't, (a) I might think there is no reason and you just enjoy throwing your weight around, or (b) what I imagine is probably worse than the truth."

Nature abhors a vacuum. So does human nature. We all want to know the *why* behind the *what*. Sometimes we try to figure out *why* even before there is a *what*.

Openness reduces vacuum pressure. When we conceal, intentionally or unintentionally, we create an information vacuum that people will fill. When our youngest daughter turned sixteen, she went a little dark on me. I couldn't do anything right. Finally, I asked if she could help me be a better parent for her. She said, "Yes, you could trust me." I had no idea what she was talking about. Evidently, when I gave her the same house rules I had given the first two kids, I left out the "why." She filled the information vacuum by thinking I didn't trust her. Nothing could have been further from the truth. Like most of us, my daughter didn't fill in the "why" question with sweet thoughts.

It is human nature to make attributions, and it is probably our fallen human nature that tilts us toward cynical attributions. Shortly after I arrived at Whitworth we decided to make a change in our benefits program. It was a no-brainer. We were adding choices to the plan. I expected high fives from all the employees, but aside from a few polite gestures, suspicion ruled the day. Had we laid out our plans openly, sought employees' perspectives before making our decision, and then announced what was coming, people would have been grateful rather than suspicious. Unless we are intentionally and explicitly open, we invite suspicion rather than understanding.

My dad was great, but he didn't see transparency anywhere in his job description as a parent, especially when it involved money. We weren't allowed to ask anybody how much something cost, how much they tithed, or, heaven forbid, how much they made. He thought it was rude. I'm sure he was right, and I learned my lesson well, so it was years before I started asking myself, "Why shouldn't the people where I work know my salary? If I were the CEO of a publicly held company, the whole world would know what I make. Shouldn't the Christian institution I lead be as transparent on this issue as the rest of the world?" Now, the federal government has forced nonprofit organizations to disclose, but it is interesting to ask why our openness had to be mandated.

History will record the first five years of this century as among the most scandalous the business world has ever seen. Personal and corporate greed festered in dens of secrecy. As empires crumbled, gross misrepresentations were exposed. Eventually, the government stepped in with legislation—the now famous Sarbanes-Oxley Act—where ethics had failed. And thus transparency shifted from a virtue to a law; openness ceased to be seen as simply a wise business practice and became an expensive regulation.

TRANSPARENCY, VALUES, AND RULES

Organizational theorist Richard Barrett argues in his book, *Building a Value-Driven Organization* (Butterworth-Heinemann, 2006), that the best organizations live by their values. Clearly, value-driven organizations outperform rule-driven organizations. Two weeks ago, I went to a post office to return a package that got mangled in shipping. I was told I had to go to a different post office to get an approval. I asked the attendant if she had any doubt that my request would be approved. She said no. I asked her if she had the capacity to return the package. She said yes. I asked her if she believed the sign behind her that listed customer satisfaction as the number-one priority. She said yes. I said I was an unsatisfied customer and I asked her to satisfy me by doing what she was sure the other post office would do. She said no, it was against the rules. I asked her if she wished she worked for a company that trusted her good judgment. She didn't know what to say. I went to the proper post office. I am now an ex-customer.

Decisions based on values (like customer satisfaction) rely on wisdom and honesty. Rules depend on knowledge and obedience. Value-driven organizations benefit from the access to information enabled by openness. Rule-driven organizations need only enough information to enforce the rules.

To be sure, we need rules. Rules codify our highest values. They give order to organizational life. They answer questions. They give boundaries that keep us from drifting outside of core values. There are some aspects of organizational life that benefit more from consistency than from adaptation. No organization can function without the rules and policies that reflect its core values. I am pro rules. I just think they should be a last resort.

The best leaders want thinkers in their organizations. Less talent is needed to obey a rule than to make a well-reasoned decision. When a rule takes judgment out of the hands of well-trained people, both their enthusiasm and their creativity atrophies. Most of us who have ever shopped at Seattle-based Nordstrom have stories to tell about the department store's elevation of honesty and good judgment over rules. Each new Nordstrom employee gets the rule book on a five-by-seven-inch index card that reads:

We're glad to have you with our Company. Our number-one goal is to provide outstanding customer service. Set both your personal and professional goals high. We have great confidence in your ability to achieve them.

Nordstrom Rules: Rule #1: Use your good judgment in all situations. There will be no additional rules.

They mean it. Several years ago I was scheduled to speak at 10:30 a.m. in Portland, Oregon. I flew in the night before with a suit I had picked up from the cleaners on the way to the airport. As I was getting dressed to speak, it became clear that the pants did not belong to the suit. Somehow, the cleaners had put a Spokane policewoman's trousers with my suit coat. Alas, she was not my size. I raced over to Nordstrom's where I was so animated waiting for them to open that the guy who unlocked the door literally thought I had to go to the bathroom. I asked the nearest salesperson how fast I could get a suit and have it tailored. "Normally, it takes a week, but I think we can get you out of here in under twenty-five minutes." They did.

The best leaders want thinkers in their organizations. Less talent is needed to obey a rule than to make a well-reasoned decision.

Values are smarter than rules, and when leaders convert organizational values into rules, they are left with restrictors rather than guides. Back to King Darius. Daniel spent the night with lions because a rule restricted the king's judgment. The value was to respect the king. The rule was to pray to the king only. Daniel excelled at the value. It was the rule that betrayed him.

Unfortunately, most rules originate because of bad judgment. Rather than teach our people how to make wise decisions, we make another rule. This past summer I spoke with a man who told me his company's "policy handbook" is, and I quote, "a history of our company's screwups. Behind every policy and rule, I was able to trace disasters big and small. Now, policies are more responsible for running the business than people."

Few leaders would argue that it is easier to impose a disclosure rule than it is to build transparency into the organizational culture. A culture of transparency emerges from the example of the leaders and from messages of reinforcement: "I really appreciate this information; thanks for copying me on this email; this is the kind of information that is so helpful; I didn't know that; thanks for including the background behind this decision."

I'm stunned with the way most Christian organizations exalt their rules. With great pride they point to their boundaries. But when a community is defined by its boundaries, or rules, rather than by the heart those rules protect, its identity becomes who *it is not* rather than who *it is*. How many times have we heard Christians described as "they're the people who don't . . . ." For example, how do we think of the Amish community? By their rules — nonviolence and no electricity. But after the horrifying 2006 murder of five little girls at a Pennsylvania schoolhouse we saw a different perspective. Before the families had lowered five handcrafted wooden caskets into the ground, they began the difficult work of forgiving the suicide-murderer and starting a fund to aid his widow and three children. The world that knew the Amish only by their rules was shocked by their heart, a heart that revealed them to be more about the love and forgiveness of Christ.

A culture of openness helps keep us attached to what drives us, rather than to how we regulate ourselves. When we live openly in a church or any other organization, we ask questions, we seek advice, we think out loud, we enlist help. Openness brings our mission and core values to the surface. Mission-driven churches, ministries, and businesses thrive in a culture of openness. Rule-driven bureaucracies require obedience. If people obey, openness is optional. It doesn't improve decision making.

TRANSPARENCY AND INTEGRITY

Openness is not only Christlike, but a commitment to openness is a commitment to truth. In June of 2006, a call was made to the Washington, D.C., police from a sales agent for the Dutch financial company, ING. Someone had broken into his house and stolen several personal items, including his laptop with the names and social security numbers of thirteen thousand District of Columbia employees. Unfortunately, the information was not encrypted. About a month later I had an opportunity to have lunch with Kathy Murphy, the ING CEO in the U.S., so I asked her how she responded to the mess. "I went to D.C. and we immediately took responsibility for not protecting the data. We notified every person affected and offered to pay for one year of credit monitoring and identity fraud protection." When I asked her how they made the decisions that ended up winning the approval of the D.C. police department, she referenced the company's culture of transparency. "It wasn't a big decision. We have a very transparent culture and we just told the truth."

Whenever I hear stories like this, I cringe a little because we've seen too many examples in the Christian community where the truth gets

PRACTICAL STEPS TO GUARD YOUR PERSONAL INTEGRITY

1. Ask your director of information systems to check your computer's "footprints" on a regular basis, to see which websites you've visited.
2. Give your spouse and your executive assistant your computer password.
3. Ask a subordinate to review each expense report before you submit it.
4. Whenever possible, travel with someone.
5. When you check into a hotel, request that the adult channels be blocked from your television.

shaded or concealed. Perhaps we feel that our calling and kingdom goals provide us with spin license. I received a letter from a well-respected Christian organization that claimed to be relocating an operation. Please send money. In truth, they were closing their current program and reopening a very different (downsized) model in a different place. It wasn't an out-and-out lie, but it wasn't the truth. I could only infer that they decided a half-truth would attract more support than the truth. Might not that approach enjoy some level of amnesty because it was for the Lord's work and not personal gain? No. The Lord doesn't need us to cut moral corners in order to accomplish his purposes. I did have a chance to speak with the leaders of the organization and, to their credit, they changed the language they used to characterize the move. Investors deserve accurate information, regardless of whether the investment is in a business or a ministry. Perhaps we should go through every piece of printed literature our church or company distributes and ask: Is anything in this piece misleading?

I grew up with one of the seven victims who died from the 1982 Tylenol poisoning, so I kept a pretty close eye on the case. Parent company Johnson & Johnson first learned of the catastrophe when a reporter called from a press conference in which a Chicago medical examiner reported that Tylenol seemed to be common to several of the deaths. Company chairman James Burke immediately alerted the nation to stop taking all Tylenol products and soon after recalled every Tylenol capsule in America. Before they knew whether the company bore any fault in what turned out to be an act of evil by a sadistic person or group, they shut down the sales of their biggest and most profitable product line.

I tell this story not because Johnson & Johnson boasts a more open climate than the next company. I tell it because it illustrates how the inconvenience and expense of openness, honesty, transparency, and disclosure involves less risk than concealment, whether malicious or benign. The business world credited the makers of Tylenol for putting the safety of others above their own profits. They have become the case study in what it means to act with integrity in crisis situations. We should never allow "cost" to become a rationale for not fixing a mistake. Like few other corporate commitments, openness promotes and safeguards the kind of organizations people trust.

What happens when our organizations get hit with really bad news? A sexual harassment charge gets leveled; the treasurer gets caught with her hand in the till; E. coli is discovered in food you have served; you find tainted funds from a donor for your new sanctuary. We don't lie about these kinds of things, but *how* do we tell the truth? How soon? How completely? Too many times the truth either comes out in installments, which erodes trust, or it is spun in such a way to save face, which usually means incomplete truth.

Shortly after arriving at Whitworth I was faced with a painful, embarrassing discovery. On the morning after a joyous commencement, I sat down with the *Wall Street Journal*. Gracing the front page was a dotted picture of a man I knew, the president of Philadelphia-based New Era Foundation. I realized I was about to become really happy or really sad. I wasn't happy. The article exposed this organization that had given us net contributions of roughly $350,000 as being a philanthropic Ponzi scheme, which was now bankrupt. As I read the story, it became clear that our funds had come from other scammed Christian organizations, not from investments or from big, secret donors. When I met with our CFO, Tom Johnson, we looked each other in the eye and made a fast decision. Maybe we wanted to hurry up before we changed our mind. We agreed we would tell the whole story and send our $350,000 to the bankruptcy judge. It was the right thing to do, but it also turned out to be a beneficial thing to do. We received sympathy and support from our employees. Bilked Christian organizations heard the news that we had returned the money before the bankruptcy judge had made a decision of how to handle net positive institutions. We received letters of gratitude and compliments for our integrity. Foolishly, we had accepted money from an organization that was fiercely nontransparent. But coming clean — quickly, transparently, and completely — seemed to restore more trust than the cover we might have gotten from excuses and spin.

TRANSPARENCY AND PERSONAL ACCOUNTABILITY

In some ways, it's easier to demand openness from our organizations than from ourselves. What do we do when no one is watching, or at least when we think no one is watching? For most leaders, someone usually is. I've heard integrity defined as "what a person does when no one is looking." It's hard to deny that we feel greater temptation to breach our standards of honesty and consistency when the bright light of accountability goes dark. Well, here's a thought: keep the light on. Paul calls it not making provision for "the flesh" or sin (Romans 13:14 KJV).

I am not implying that integrity requires openness. Some leaders maintain the highest levels of integrity while functioning quite privately in their personal and professional lives. But openness does *encourage* integrity. When Christian leaders subject themselves to visibility and accountability, they reduce dramatically the likelihood of moral or ethical compromises. Leaders whose assistants always know their whereabouts will likely be smart in choosing "where they are about."

Leaders whose assistants always know their whereabouts will likely be smart in choosing "where they are about."

We can all take measures to "keep the light on." Positions of leadership often require travel, and travel has gotten brutal. By the time I arrive at my destination, I'm a wreck. Agitated, alone in a distant city, feeling deprived at having to be absent from my family, and needing relief from the indignities of air travel, I'm not at the height of my moral strength. So when I fire up my computer, I find myself tempted to click my way from e-mail to e-crap. But I don't. And one of the reasons I don't is because I have given permission to our information technology people to check the logs of the websites I've visited without notifying me. Do that and you'll think twice before you click on garbage. (Incidentally, a surprising number of people in leadership fail to realize their organizations can track down every website they've ever visited.) I've also found that the deprivations of travel can tempt me to live more luxuriously on my business expense account than I would on my own money. Personally, I don't think that's right, so I've welcomed people to review my expense reports if they have questions. Whether our temptations are prompted by travel or by other conditions, the accountability of openness can only help us be the people of integrity God calls us to be.

Hedging our weaknesses, harnessing our strengths, and wearing a life jacket even though we know how to swim are marks of prudence, not pessimism. There is no dishonor in admitting our need for help. Even a moral exemplar like Billy Graham protected himself. He never allowed himself to be alone in a room with a woman. He created a team and kept the members close at hand. According to Dr. Graham, team members served each other as friends, helpers, and moral centurions. Every leader should submit to strict accountability measures. If we don't have a "team" at our hip, giving permission, passwords, and access might be a smart way to keep the light on. It might even save a career.

Leaders drive long and hard. Our guards slip incrementally, and soon we're easy prey. Openness helps us notice when we're sliding, because if we don't see it, others will. I can be excessive, I'm a good rationalizer, I have a work hard – play hard mentality, and I can be dumb. But I shudder at the thought of letting down those whom I have been called to lead. So I try to stay in the light.

Part of the challenge of maintaining openness and accountability is due to the reality that most leaders live crowded lives. Jesus came down from the mountainside to minister to others, but he first went up to the mountainside to be alone with his Father. Christian leaders need time alone, and they need time alone with God. We live under a cosmic magnifying glass. People are watching, and everything looks bigger. I actually live where I work. I go to sleep each night with thirteen hundred college students — although my nocturnal patterns fall about three or four time zones east of theirs. Leaders, particularly those in higher profile posts, feel very accountable and very exposed. We need our privacy. Our survival requires brackets of solitude, and it is in those times of being completely alone for our restoration and renewal that we can stumble.

Great leaders have fallen in dimly lit corridors that took them to a different place than they intended to go. Satan didn't dangle temptations before Jesus in the temple. He got Jesus in the wilderness of being alone. But Jesus wasn't alone. And neither are we. The same One who was tempted stands with us and for us. He knows our infirmities, he was tempted as we are tempted, and yet he never yielded. The victor over every temptation now serves as both our high priest and our companion. We benefit greatly from openness, accountability, and transparency, but cannot allow ourselves to forget that we are never truly alone.

Satan didn't dangle temptations before Jesus in the temple. He got Jesus in the wilderness of being alone. But Jesus wasn't alone. And neither are we.

THE PARADOX OF OPENNESS

A few months ago I spoke about leadership to our state senate Democratic caucus. When they invited me, they didn't realize there would be so many of them. The election fattened their numbers considerably; so they were in a good mood. Because it wasn't a public meeting, they gave me the green light to "include your spiritual stuff if you want to." I did. Who could resist telling a bunch of happy politicians about Jesus? So, among other things, I told them how Jesus opened himself to the disciples and that they should take a lesson. I hailed transparency. I cheered for openness. I knew they would dig this stuff. Well, most of them did, but one senator pulled me aside and told me I was either nuts or naïve or both. I think I might have overstated my case, because he really nailed me on my insistence that politicians should be so transparent. And at certain points, he was absolutely right.

Knowing how much or how little to disclose is seldom clear. In the New Era Foundation case I cited earlier, we knew where we drew the disclosure line was important. We had no intention of hiding any numbers or facts, but it got a little cloudier when it came to how we got involved. Everything done was board-approved, but some board members had more influence than others. Measuring influence gets complicated and even a bit dangerous for the people involved, so we drew the information line at the point of reporting that our actions had board approval.

Sometimes, disclosing too much can do more damage than disclosing too little. So we lean toward playing it safe. But what we fail to realize is that when we dole out information too cautiously, the chances of surprising people skyrocket, and it is the surprise factor that creates an impression of duplicity. We need to build cultures of openness, but we also need to recognize that Christian organizations are fraught with delicate complexities that defy full explanation or disclosure.

Jesus dwelt with his followers. He closed the gap. He allowed them to behold him. He let them see him up close and personal. Most of us begin our careers wanting to be the same type of leader, but as we ascend the leadership mountain, we find a lot of reasons to stay up there. Jesus never led from the mountain. He came down and walked with common, ordinary people. He surrounded himself with twelve close friends, and he lived with them openly. He showed us that truly great leaders are transparent leaders.

Questions for Reflection and Discussion

1. How much behind-the-scenes information from your organization is made available to constituents (for examples, minutes from all meetings, salary information of leaders/staff, results of health or building inspections, financial audit)? What information should be withheld and why?
2. Are Christian organizations more or less likely to disclose bad news or unflattering information about themselves than secular organizations? Why or why not?
3. When you travel alone on business, what temptations do you face? How do you protect yourself from those temptations?
4. The author contends that the higher up you are as a leader, the greater opportunity you have to operate in the dark. Do you agree or disagree? Why or why not?
5. Jesus surrounded himself with twelve men who were with him almost constantly. Who are the people in your life who see you in all situations and have been encouraged to confront you if you do anything that raises concerns for them? Can you point to one example where someone close to you called you out on something? Describe.

3

Bending the Light

I tell you the truth, the Son can do nothing by himself; he can do only what he sees his Father doing, because whatever the Father does the Son also does.

John 5:19

... my power [strength] is made perfect in weakness ...

2 Corinthians 12:9

... his glory, the glory of the only begotten of the Father ...

John 1:14 KJV

Author Robert Fulghum tells the story of one of his professors, Alexander Papaderos, a very wise man from whom Fulghum once took a two-week seminar on Greek culture. At the end of the final session, his teacher asked if there were any parting questions. Bravely, Fulghum asked, "Dr. Papaderos, what is the meaning of life?" After a few moments Papaderos pulled his wallet from his pocket, removed a tiny, quarter-sized mirror, and replied:

> When I was a small child, during the war, we were very poor and we lived in a remote village. One day, on the road, I found the broken pieces of a mirror. A German motorcycle had been wrecked in that place.

> I tried to find all the pieces and put them together, but it was not possible, so I kept only the largest piece. This one. And by scratching it on a stone, I made it round. I began to play with it as a toy and became fascinated by the fact that I could reflect light into dark places where the sun would never shine — in deep holes and crevices and dark closets. It became a game for me to get light into the most inaccessible places I could find.
>
> I kept the little mirror, and as I went about my growing up, I would take it out in idle moments and continue the challenge of the game. As I became a man, I grew to understand that this was not just a child's game but a metaphor for what I might do with my life. I came to understand that I am not the light or the source of light. But light — truth, understanding, knowledge — is there, and it will only shine in many dark places if I reflect it. (*It Was on Fire When I Lay It Down* [Random House, 1992], p. 170)

Jesus *reflected* glory. We tend to *absorb* glory.We must carry an abiding awareness that we are not the light, we only reflect it. It's not about our brightness and how good we are, but about God's brightness and how good he is. Our job is to keep the mirror angled between God and darkness. Pride turns the mirror back on ourselves. We gaze at our own reflections and fool ourselves into thinking that others find us as attractive as we find ourselves. We become Narcissus until we drown in the pool of self-absorption. I love Thomas Merton's words about the glory mirrored in God's creation:

> I am abashed, solitary, helpless, surrounded by a beauty that can never belong to me. But this sadness generates within me an unspeakable reverence for the holiness of created things, for they are pure and perfect and they belong to God and they are mirrors of His beauty. He is mirrored in all things like sunlight in a clean water: but if I try to drink the light that is in the water I only shatter the reflection. (*A Year with Thomas Merton: Daily Meditations from His*

Journals, by Thomas Merton and Jonathan Montaldo [HarperOne, 2004], p. 259)

May God keep us from trying to drink the sunlight that is Christ. We cannot absorb the glory that belongs to him without troubling the waters and distorting the reflection of his beauty, truth, and grace.

IT'S NOT ABOUT ME

If anyone had the right to say, "It's all about me," it was Jesus. But he didn't. He said, "It's all about my Father who sent me; it's all about my mission. I'm here to serve." Taking on the likeness of sinful man should have exempted Jesus from having to perform any further acts of humility. What's left after moving from heaven to Nazareth? But Jesus exemplified humility. Jesus exalted humility. Jesus exuded humility. And Jesus was the only person ever literally to embody humility.

Taking on the likeness of sinful man should have exempted Jesus from having to perform any further acts of humility. What's left after moving from heaven to Nazareth?

The glory of Jesus was a reflected glory. Trinitarian mysteries conceal the exact nature of the divine father-son relationship, but John clearly linked the glory of Jesus with that of his Father. So did Jesus. Unflinchingly, he deflected credit. In an ingenious defense of his work on the Sabbath (John 5:1 – 15), Jesus would not allow the Jewish leaders to designate him as the source of divine power; his miracles, he explained, came from the Father:

> *I tell you the truth, the Son can do nothing by himself; he can do only what he sees his Father doing, because whatever the Father does the Son also does. (John 5:19)*

In John Calvin's comments on this passage (*Commentary on John, vol. 6*), he says: "We ought always to keep in remembrance that, whenever Christ speaks concerning himself, he claims only that which belongs to man ... he ascribes to the Father whatever is higher than man."

When I was a graduate student I had a professor whom I loved and still do. One day he divided up our class into pairs, and because we had an odd number of students, I ended up as his partner for the exercise. Our task was to trade sentences that began with "I am." I remember how surprised I was when my young, gifted professor Em Griffin offered his first statement: "I am a rich man through no doing of my own." What I heard was, "I have wealth that I didn't earn." Every Christian leader could say the same thing. Where would we be without God's redeeming grace, our families of origin, and the gifts God gave us? And we earned none of these. But I still catch myself inviting everyone to admire my accomplishments rather than God's amazing grace. Recently I ran across something that I wrote on my tenth anniversary as a college president. I should paste this to the inside of my eyelids and read it every time I bat them.

> Leading is not about me. Letting go of my recognition, my image, my control and my self-interest will free me to grasp my responsibility. My duty is to see that this college executes its mission with excellence and strength. Any needs I have to be the star of that execution steal from Whitworth and misdirect my energy. When I let go of my pride, my role changes. I become the server rather than the served. If I stick to my self-concept of strategist, interpreter, and cheerleader, I think I can survive this job for a few more years. But if everything's all about me, I will buckle under the weight of my own frailties and needs. It's too hard to keep my ego fed. The more it gets, the more it wants.

No competitor, no incompetence, and no amount of bad luck will bring down a leader as swiftly and devastatingly as her or his ego.

OUR OKAY SIN

If Jesus carefully deflects glory to his Father and brightly reflects the glory of his Father, we might want to think twice about being glory absorbers. Some Christian leaders act like they think the Bible is just kidding in its warnings against pride. We pluck condemnations of homosexuality out of the 613 Levitical laws (most of which we ignore), add them to the relatively few (but I would say clear) New Testament prohibitions, and split our denominations over the issue. Pride, however, seems to enjoy immunity from our list of abominable sins, in spite of 119 explicit biblical warnings. Why isn't the church in as much of an uproar over pride as it is over homosexuality? I have a minister friend whose breadth of knowledge leaves me in awe. His oratorical skills are consummate, and he is nothing short of an assassin on contemporary evils. But when he confesses what he calls his "nagging sin of pride," he sighs lightheartedly. He seems to accept it as the cross of one so gifted. But I don't think God accepts it. What makes us think God gets mad about homosexuality but he's a good sport about pride? Pride is wrong. I hate it. I have it. It hurts my leadership. It hurts my marriage. It hurts everything. I don't want it. God doesn't want me to have it. And I should get mad when I get proud.

John's description of Jesus as a reflector of God the Father's glory offers the key for leaders who struggle with pride ... and that would be most of us. We need to think of ourselves as reflectors. We shine the light of Christ's grace and truth on those we lead. And we reflect any credit we receive back to Christ, the giver of every good and perfect gift. Mirrors reflect in both directions, and Christ shines infinitely more on us than we shine on him.

I have found three "pride-checks" to be helpful in almost every situation:

- How would I respond if this situation had absolutely no bearing on how I am perceived?

- If I were a consultant, how would I advise someone else to respond in this situation?
- What response would bend the light toward others?

BECOMING A MIRROR

In my first year as a college president, a trustee suggested that I send a letter to a man suggesting he make a gift. So I did. The man replied that he did have a little stock he would give to the college. When I went to see him I discovered that "little" meant a $168,000 gift. In my circles, that's a major gift, and I was giddy over what had dropped out of the sky because of a perceptive trustee. When I told a president-friend, he said, "Nice job!" I replied that I had nothing to do with it other than show up and take the money. He responded with, "Look, presidents get unwarranted blame when something bad happens on their watch; they should also get the credit for the good stuff that happens." I don't agree.

When we deflect praise toward others, the recipients feel great. They deserve the recognition, and we deplete none of our own. It's as though the bounce off us leaves a mark, a very good mark. When we steal praise, everyone suffers, ourselves included. I once worked with an administrator whose leadership was proving very ineffective. After we sifted out all the little things, it became clear that this person let his needs for recognition overshadow the needs of the people he led. The first time he co-opted credit for another person's accomplishments, the group cut him some slack. The second time they asked me to cut him from the team. People will penalize hubris in leadership.

I am better at describing a mirror than at being one. I want to reflect Christ's light, but I allow people to make me the light. Leaders are often the focal point for credit, even though it takes many people working together for an organization to succeed. When Whitworth University gets an award, it's often handed to me, even though I am seldom the reason we got it. I was once credited publicly for our football team's 10–0 record. More absurd credit has never been given, but I still rather liked it.

Further, it's not just the fact that other people make me feel as if I'm the light. Often, I make myself the light. Way too many times my wife has caught me changing the subject in order to bring the conversation closer to whatever it is I want to use to make myself look good. So, I've got nothing to brag about when it comes to humility.

For me, Christ's table brings me to my knees in a way nothing else does. Mystically, no taste favors my tongue like the peculiar combination of plain white bread soaked in grape juice. At the table, I am blunted with penetrating awareness that I am not worthy but Christ is so worthy, worthy enough to present me faultless before the living God. I imagine Jesus kneeling with a basin at the disciples' feet and I am flooded with cleansing shame. I hear the words of John the Baptist, "I am not worthy to untie his sandal." My duty is a gift — the unspeakable privilege of reflecting this man who stooped. My only credential for being a mirror is his mercy.

I would urge every Christian leader to feast regularly at Christ's table, to find a way to live into this sacrament. Jesus said, "For as *often* as you eat this bread and drink this cup," not "for as *seldom* as you eat ... and drink." Whether we serve Christ as pastors or laypeople, we would benefit from pursuing Christ's supper, rather than just letting it come to us. I've asked my pastor for communion as a congregation of one. It is at the table I reckon with the horror of my pride as I remember the humility and humiliation of my Savior. It is there I feel most palpably I have entered into Christ's presence.

My duty is a gift — the unspeakable privilege of reflecting this man who stooped. My only credential for being a mirror is his mercy.

A reflector has one main job — to reflect. When Christian leaders present an image that doesn't reflect Christ, they've often inserted their own picture onto the reflecting pane. To credit ourselves with God's gifts and blessings distorts and conceals the truth. To reflect Christ's glory is to obey his commandments; to forgive, as we have been forgiven; to love, not hate; to be generous with everything we have; to proclaim his gospel in word and deed; to be humble, not haughty. It is to be Christlike in a thorough and glorious list of ways that blessedly and arduously go on and on. This is what we preach to our followers. Is it how we live as leaders?

HUMILITY'S ALLY—TRUTH

Another way leaders can keep from wearing those jerseys of darkness that absorb the light is to put on the bright reflecting colors of truth. If God got nothing more out of Christian leaders than the truth, he'd probably consider it progress. Truth protects against pride because truth recognizes that every gift comes from the God. Truth recognizes grace as the means of our salvation and nothing about which we can boast. Truth recognizes that the mirror is but a mirror; it's not the object it reflects.

Truth also competes against a besetting tendency of Christian leaders: We like to spiritualize our accomplishments. When we attribute a success to God, report why God gave the success, and claim we had nothing to do with the success, we're speculating. We don't know the mind and motives of God. "'My thoughts are not your thoughts, neither are your ways my ways,' declares the LORD" (Isaiah 55:8). Further, our efforts do play a role in what we achieve. The truth is that when we do the work, God gives the increase. Scripture connects labor with fruit; if you do the former, you get the latter. That connection doesn't give us bragging rights; it simply acknowledges that God uses flawed people to accomplish his purposes.

Excessively spiritualizing success opens two doors to pride. First, claiming we are nothing inspires others to think we are too humble, so they praise us not only for our achievements but for our humility. Second, when we really think we know the what and the why of God's ways, pride can't be far behind. Christian leaders must be careful about speaking for God. People can hear the opinions and interpretations of Christians in positions of authority as straight from the Bible, and the likelihood of confusion rises when the expressions are particularly spiritual or pious.

Even prefacing our declarations with phrases such as "I really believe the reason God ..." carries a risk. If people perceive those of us in leadership as believing we know the mind of God, they will idolize us or dismiss us. Both are bad. When Pat Robertson and Jerry Falwell claimed the terrorist attacks of September 11 were punishments from God, too many people believed them unquestioningly or dismissed them as goofballs. Clearly, God breaks into our lives in wonderful and sobering ways, but we shouldn't present our interpretation of God's intervention with the same truth tones we use to present the clear truths of Scripture.

Undoubtedly, a leader's pride can contribute to the confusion of truth and opinion. Pastors and ministry leaders are thrust into positions of leadership because they declare the truth. That's great! But then pride begins to take over and the sequence reverses itself. These leaders start to believe that something is true because they declare it. We need to stick to the truth. Maybe God did put me in seat 33C because the guy in 33B was depressed. Maybe God did prompt him to start up a conversation with me. Frankly, it would be just like God to do that. But I'm not God. I don't know all the reasons I'm in 33C, and I need to be careful about declaring what God did and didn't do. Here's what I do know as the truth of God's Word: I know it is true that I should praise God for every opportunity to proclaim Christ's gospel; I know it is true that the depressed guy next to me is made in the image of God; and I know it is true that my Christian duty is to show him the love of Christ in every way possible.

Truth enjoys greater protection from humility than from pride.

WHAT HUMILITY ISN'T

Just because we are humble doesn't mean we are timid. As leaders, we ought to push, hustle, compete, and run with the abandon of those who have heard the high call to follow Christ. Humility taps into the recognition that we're not good enough to rest on our laurels. When we humbly give our efforts to Christ, we insult him if they are meager efforts. Arrogance breeds laziness; humility energizes. We've been bought with a high price. Our owner deserves to have us drive hard.

Scripture's references to importunate prayer offer a theology of humble aggressiveness. In the Old Testament, Isaiah takes on the voice of God urging "You who call on the LORD, give yourselves no rest." If that isn't enough, he goes further and says, "And give him no rest" (Isaiah 62:6–7). God wants us to stay after him. Jesus picks up the theme in his parable of the guy who needed three loaves of bread and pounded on his friend's door at midnight. Jesus makes the strange but clear observation that aggressiveness more than friendship will produce the bread.

We've been bought with a high price. Our owner deserves to have us drive hard.

It bears reminding that pushing and driving in obedience to God does not mean we will get our way. The results of our persistence lie in God's sovereign hands, not ours. A few nights ago I watched a TV pastor tell the story of a man who kept praying for new furniture. And when the man's son hauled off and won $37 million in the lottery, he not only got the furniture but a new house to put it in. There are about a bazillion things I find appalling about suggesting that the guy prayed his way into the jackpot, but mostly I don't like the implication that our prayers *determine* the results of God's grace.

This connection between prayer and the lottery might have struck me more charitably had a small army of friends and I not spent months praying for a dear saint named Walt who just lost his battle to cancer. We prayed hard because we loved Walt, and God tells us to come after him with our prayers. I suppose the fortunate new home owner may also have petitioned God out of simple obedience to Christ. Good for him. But bad for any Christian leader implying (a) the persistency of our prayers will get us the answer we want, and (b) God answered his prayer with a gambling mechanism that has deepened the poverty of millions of poor Americans who exchange their meager funds for the false hope of getting something for nothing. Finally, bad for me if I'm saying God couldn't use whatever means he pleases to accomplish his purposes. What we know for sure is that God wants us to reflect Christ's humility while working and praying fervently. The kind of assertiveness that tells God what to do, or speaks for God, brings God's ways down to our ways. That's never a good deal for God or for us.

Humility coupled with aggressiveness comes in a lot of different flavors. Some Christian leaders plug away relentlessly but without a lot of wasted movement. They plow through to-do lists big and small with persistence and endurance, staying on a pretty straight path. For three years as his underling, I watched Rev. Woody Strodel work this way. He reminded me of Aesop's tortoise, serving an impressive cast of legendary senior pastor hares: John Ockenga, James Kennedy, John Huffman, Clayton Bell, Ron Scates. Quietly, steadfastly, and effectively, Woody used his abundant gifts to support the legendary ministries of these great, high-profile pastors. I remember a staff meeting where John Huffman asked all nine of us to report what we most wanted in life. I don't remember what I or anybody else answered ... except for Woody, who said, "I want to be faithful." That's the battle cry of the leader who unites aggressiveness and humility.

SUBMITTING OURSELVES TO THE MISSION

In one of the most fascinating organizational studies ever conducted, leadership titan Jim Collins introduced the world of management and leadership to the "Level 5" leader. After sifting through more than 1,500 companies that had appeared on the Fortune 500 over a thirty-year period, he found eleven matched pairs that met his criteria, which he recounted in his bestselling book *Good to Great: Why Some Companies*

Make the Leap ... And Others Don't (Collins, 2001). Half the companies had gone from good to great, and half made no such move. The characteristic Collins cited as most dominant in the leaders of the companies achieving greatness was a blend of extreme personal humility and intense professional will. These Level 5 leaders were extraordinarily aggressive, but their humility enabled them to invest in the strength of their teammates, yield their personal desires to the mission of the company, and give rather than grab credit. In two-thirds of the other companies, Collins found leaders with "gargantuan" egos.

In the January 3, 2006 issue of *Management Issues*, Stuart Crainer interviewed Collins. When asked to define the Level 5 leader, Collins replied:

> It came down to one essential definition. The central dimension for Level 5 is a leader who is ambitious first and foremost for the cause, for the company, for the work, not for himself or herself; and has an absolutely terrifying iron will to make good on that ambition. It is that combination, the fact that *it is not about them, it's not first and foremost for them, it is for the company* and its long-term interests, of which they are just a part. But it is not a meekness; it is not a weakness; it is not a wallflower type. It's the other side of the coin.... They will do whatever it takes to make the company great. No matter how painful, no matter how emotionally stressing the decision has to be, they have the will to do it. It is that very unusual combination, which separates out the Level 5 leaders. [italics mine]

In essence, Collins argues for leaders reflecting rather than usurping the glory of their company's mission and performance. Apparently, the business world has discovered the power of humility and the truth of Christ's example and teachings. As Christian leaders we need to channel our ambitions for the glory of God, not for ourselves.

Collins's Level 5 leaders start with the mission rather than a preconceived program or strategy for which they can claim credit. *Is the mission noble? Does it reflect the core values of who we are and why we exist? How are we contributing to the greater good?* As ministries, we can ill afford fuzzy, overly general mission statements. We need a shared understanding of what God is calling us to do. Our mission should be clear and defining.

Once the mission has been established and embraced, we work backwards with the "accomplish" questions. *Are these operations the most efficient and effective way to accomplish the mission? How does this program help accomplish the mission? Is this opportunity consistent with the mission?* Successful organizations walk the fine line between adaptability and mission drift; it's the difference between being innovative and being lost.

HOW TO SPREAD THE GLOW

Here are six practical ways to share the spotlight:

1. Begin the practice of trying to "catch" your subordinates doing something right and recognize them for their accomplishments.
2. Rotate the leadership of your weekly staff meetings among your associates.
3. When the media requests an interview, include at least one other associate in the interview.
4. Invite an associate to accompany you on a business trip. It's a great way to mentor your leaders and further protects you from the temptations of the road.
5. Regularly devote some time in staff meetings for your associates to respond to the question, "How can I serve you and our mission more effectively?" Then listen.
6. Delegate important assignments, then support them without micromanaging.

One of the great warnings of mission drift came in the frighteningly prescient 1999 book written by Hofstra University professor Robert Sobel, *When Giants Stumble: Classic Business Blunders and How to Avoid Them.* The scary formula emerging from Sobel's research is that highly successful businesses are vulnerable to the kind of hubris that believes "we can make anything work." When we start to consider ourselves, more than our missions, as the reason for success, disaster is just around the corner. Jesus always understood the concept of "mission first." The first time Scripture records him getting in trouble with his parents (although I rather think it was not the first time), he explains he was on mission; he was "about my Father's business" (Luke 2:49 KJV).

THE STRENGTH OF HUMILITY

Just because Jesus had extraordinary humility did not mean he backed away. One of the most intense stories in the Gospels, recorded in Luke 6, finds Jesus standing up to the Pharisees in the synagogue. He had already outraged them by "working" on the Sabbath. Now, they had gathered on another Sabbath in hopes of catching him again. As Jesus teaches, he sees a man with a shriveled hand. "Get up and stand in front of everyone," he says. A proud Jesus might have turned to the Pharisees and sneered, "Watch this." But the humble and brave Jesus simply asks which is lawful on the Sabbath: to do good or evil. He then heals the man's hand. And that did it for the Pharisees. They began plotting to kill him. Jesus could not have been more humble, but he did not waver or compromise.

The synagogue showdown between Jesus and the Pharisees reminds us that humility does not mean weakness. Jesus stood his ground. He put his personal comfort and safety on the line. In fact, humility in leadership builds strength.

One of world's best examples of humility and strength united has a familiar ring. He dressed like a commoner, served his friends, condemned violence, and willingly suffered for his people. Jesus? No, but it was a man who patterned his life after Jesus—Mahatma Gandhi, whom history credits with liberating India from British colonialism. Graham Standish, Presbyterian pastor and author of *Humble Leadership: Being Radically Open to God's Guidance and Grace*, writes:

> Gandhi led from a strength rooted in humility, and I learned a lot from his example. I learned that there is strength in humility, and that humble leadership exposes self-interest and selfishness in both enemies and friends alike, as it simultaneously purifies motives. When we lead from a sense of humility, willingly putting aside our own motivations and desires in favor of God's call, we create the context in which people are more willing to put aside their own will to seek God's will. (*Congregations*, Spring 2007, No. 2)

Gandhi's story demonstrates how leadership strength borne of humility comes not simply from self-abasement but from stationing the good of our people in front of our self-interest, self-comfort, and self-gratification. In South Africa Gandhi endured brutal beatings. In India he fasted for weeks on end. In Britain he denied himself common comforts. In his entire lifetime of nonviolent battles, this frail man summoned immense strength, not for his own gain but for the liberation of his people.

It is hard to imagine that Gandhi would have found strength to do for himself what he was strong enough to do for his people. I think humans carry a reservoir of strength that can be tapped only in service of others. When people (even unregenerate people) follow God's truth, they find a power unavailable to those (even Christians) who follow the lies of pride.

Years ago I read about a basketball coach who took a team of Christian players to Argentina for a series of games over the Christmas holidays (Argentina's midsummer). One afternoon at the ocean beach, a wicked riptide roared in and snagged several unsuspecting players. While most scrambled to safety, the coach saw one weak swimmer losing his battle against the tidal forces. So he went after his player. Somehow, in helping his player reach the human chain that would pull him to safety, the coach spent everything he had. As the new victim of the tide's pull, he tells how he felt the strange peace of resignation. He had lived life well, he would succumb without regret. But just at that point he heard the voices of his small children on the shore pleading with him not to give up. He reports that picturing them growing up without their dad, and imagining his wife grieving the loss of her husband, burst open a resolve unavailable even to a man fighting for his life. With absolutely nothing left for himself, he found a special reserve for his family. Miraculously, he traversed his way to the grip of those who would pull him into the presence of his saviors—his family. For years he battled the effects of lactic acid toxins that his body manufactured for the miracle, but his kids have a dad.

Leaders compete, even humble leaders, especially humble leaders, because they will fight for their people long after they have fought enough for themselves. Aggressive competition is not the opposite of glory-reflecting humility. The big question is not *whether* we should compete; the big questions are *for whom* and *against whom*. We compete *for* the people with whom we have been entrusted, *for* the mission to which we have been called, and *for* the One who has called us. But against whom? The nature and range of our opponents run the gamut. Friendly competition among ministries keeps us sharp. Whitworth and Seattle Pacific University share a similar mission and the same state. We compete with them for students, and we compete hard. But I love SPU, its president, students, faculty members, and the mission they represent. In

The big question is not *whether* we should compete; the big questions are *for whom* and *against whom*.

fact, I'm a donor. So, I want them to do well, but I want their success to serve as an incentive for us to be the best we can be.

Clearly, though, my biggest competitor is not another college or university. My most deadly enemy is me. I live in the terrifying acknowledgment that what Cardinal Newman wrote 150 years ago in *The Idea of a University* (1852) is as true of me as it is of any leader:

> Quarry the granite rock with razors, or moor the vessel with a thread of silk; then may you hope with such keen and delicate instruments as human knowledge and human reason to contend against those giants, the passion and the pride of man.

I lack the strength to defeat my own pride. Most of us do. That's Cardinal Newman's point. I was a child when I memorized Philippians 4:13 (NKJV): "I can do all things through Christ who strengthens me." I think my parents hoped that verse would give me self-confidence. I do need Christ's strength and I do need confidence. But I need Christ-confidence more than self-confidence. And where I need Christ's strength the most is to contend against the giants: the pride and the passion of man.

THE PARADOX OF HUMILITY

I once heard a slumping NFL quarterback moaning about how his team had lost its swagger. Lovely. Here's a game where even a routine play ends with some guy strutting around like a peacock, thumping himself on the chest, and then pointing to the sky, which probably has something to do with God. The NFL needs a lot of things, but swagger isn't one of them.

However, the quarterback was right about one thing: you can't do anything successfully without confidence. If swagger represents the NFL version of confidence, then I'm okay with it. Paradoxically, leadership requires the union of confidence and humility.

When Christians hear God's call to leadership, it comes with a promise. After Moses recited all the reasons why he was *not* confident about accepting God's call to go fetch the Israelites from Egypt, he got the promise that comes with the call. God said, "Certainly, I will be with you." Whether standing in front of a congregation, negotiating a major deal, or running a staff meeting, certainly God is with us. We have no reason to stare at our feet and mumble. Further, we should not expect those we lead to be any more confident than their leader.

So how do we, at once, lead with confidence and humility? It must be possible and important because Christ loved both qualities. In Matthew 5 he said the meek would inherit the earth. And then in Matthew 21 he tells the disciples if they had enough faith they could do a showy miracle like getting a mountain to throw itself into the sea. Apparently we can be meek and still move mountains. The question is, How?

I've thought a lot about this because at various times I struggle with both insecurity and overconfidence. Perhaps giving account of *my* struggle belies any claim to humility, but it's the struggle I know best. The first sentence of my last self-evaluation summary symbolizes the way I experience this paradox: "Some days I feel clueless, and some days I feel I can do this job better than anybody; but most days I'm too busy to feel either."

By more than eight years, I am the youngest of four children. My dad started the missionary aviation program at Moody Bible Institute where my mother served on the music faculty. My three siblings excelled in most everything, including life, which they all spent in missions while raising great families. I got off to a slow start compared to them. My dad said I was talented but lazy; my mom skipped the lazy part and relentlessly reported that she and God loved me, and I should love me too.

I couldn't have asked for better parents, and you can't love parents more than I loved mine, but Dad's shaming wasn't such a good strategy for me. If people thought I was smart without trying, why should I work hard and run the risk of proving them wrong? I remember when Dad told me I'd never be great at any sport. "When it stops being fun and you have to really work to get better, you'll just move on to the next fun thing." Rather than thinking "I'll show you," I thought, "Makes sense to me."

We were Baptists, which meant I got sermons every Sunday that seemed to vaccinate me against guilt and shame, and Dad had too much of a conscience to hit me with anything that would overpower those inoculations. But Mom's idealized view of me wasn't great either. She sowed the seeds of unwarranted confidence. Way too often I found myself underprepared for challenges, academic and otherwise. I was sure I could wing it, whatever it was. I was often less than my best. I was not the Adonis she claimed I was, not by a long shot. Actually, I think it was these dueling strategies that prompted me to tell my fifteen-year-old son, "Ben, you're a great kid with great potential, but you have some catching up to do with your self-image." He now loves reminding me of how I told him he needed lower self-esteem.

For years I would hear the voices of confidence and humility arguing with each other. Frankly, I still do. I think it might be the strategies of my parents clashing. Those messages don't bind me, but they can move the humility paradox from being one of self-perception to one of self-motivation. And when humility (or confidence) becomes tactical, rather than an authentic view of our capacity, it loses its reliability. It becomes a ploy. If we're trying to motivate or trick ourselves or others, we'll choose the most effective means, regardless of its proximity to reality. False humility falls into this category. It is often disingenuous fishing for praise.

For me to navigate the waters of the humility paradox I have had to learn that confidence and humility are not inversely related; they are not opposite ends of a continuum. The theological basis for coupling humility and confidence is clear. In humility we acknowledge our gifts are from God. We have nothing to brag about. But our gifts are from *God*. What can give more confidence than that! In humility we acknowledge our utter sinfulness. But we have been redeemed by no less than the God of the universe. In humility we recognize that God's strength is made perfect in our weakness.

The practical implication of this theological foundation gives us permission to acknowledge the limits of our capacity and the unworthiness of our condition. It's humbling. But this awareness also points us in the direction of our gifts. It reminds us that God has equipped us to succeed in whatever he calls us to do. And it also reminds us that ultimately our success is not about what we have or what we do; it is about what God has, what God has done, and what God continues to do. At once, Christians should be the most humble and confident of all people. When we are confident and not humble we deny the grace of God. When we are humble and not confident we deny the power of God. With Paul we can be "confident of this, that he who began a good work in you will carry it on to completion until the day of Christ Jesus" (Philippians 1:6).

QUESTIONS FOR REFLECTION AND DISCUSSION

1. When you deliver a successful presentation or sermon and your listeners lavish you with praise, how does that make you feel? Is such praise beneficial and necessary? How can it become toxic? How do you personally keep praise in its rightful perspective?
2. The author warns against using humility as an excuse for timid leadership, saying that great leaders are relentless competitors. Who or what are you competing against? What drives your competitiveness? How does that affect how you go about your work as a leader?
3. To date, what are you most proud of as a leader? Do you see God's hand in the accomplishment? What have you done to celebrate that accomplishment, and how can you use it to motivate others rather than cause resentment or bring attention to yourself?
4. In what area do you feel a deep awareness of God's abundant grace and, simultaneously, a deep awareness of your own ability, preparation, and effort?

4

Living in Grace and Truth

Jesus straightened up and asked her, "Woman, where are they? Has no one condemned you?" "No one, sir," she said. "Then neither do I condemn you," Jesus declared. "Go now and leave your life of sin."

John 8:10 – 11

Sometimes grace and truth are hard to sort out. Last year I got a call from our son in Cairo, Egypt. He mentioned that on his return to Egypt, he read the first book I wrote. Here's the essence of *his* grace and truth:

> "Hey, Dad, I read your book while I was in Sweden." [Although the book came out a few years earlier, that he read it at all was definitely grace.]
>
> "Yeah, I would have really liked it . . ." [Now, this is a sure sign that truth is on its way.]
>
> "I would have really liked it if I were remotely interested in the subject." [A little too much truth here.]
>
> "But it was well written." [Definitely grace.]
>
> "And I liked the parts about me." [Definitely truth.]

Grace and truth need each other. Grace ceases to be grace if it lacks truth. And truth loses its power if it lacks grace. Grace without truth sanctions and perpetuates unwanted actions. Attorneys love it when clients filing for wrongful dismissal present them with a stack of acceptable performance reviews. Is it grace when we give silent slack rather than constructive criticism to ineffective employees? Is it grace when we allow our friends or relatives to wander down dangerous paths without saying anything? No. Grace without truth is not grace at all.

But it can also be argued that truth without grace cannibalizes itself. About six months after I graduated from college I was doing youth work in a church that was divided on a very important issue. One day the main leader on one side of the issue invited me out to lunch. Not more than ten minutes into the meal, I realized that I was the lunch. After he got done chewing me up, I grunted through tears and anger the only thing that made sense to me: "I quit." Over the years, I've reflected on that encounter in search of anything that could be helpful to me. Happily, I've come up with some guidelines for people who want to pummel me with the truth:

- First, I will have a hard time hearing truth if I am busy defending myself.
- Second, I will have a hard time identifying truth if the assault feels like it's more for your good than for mine.
- Third, I am not capable of accepting truth from you if the attack feels personal.
- Fourth, I will stop thinking about truth if you make claims about my motives. Only I know my motives—and I would rather you ask me what they are than tell me what you think they are.

So for me, and I suspect every other human being in our culture, without grace you will lose credibility, and any hope for truth telling will be destroyed.

Truth without grace is harsh, usually self-centered, and very un-Christlike. Grace without truth is deceptively permissive, often lazy, and equally un-Christlike. Good leaders communicate both grace and truth in love. Loving those we lead answers the question, "Should I show grace or should I tell the truth?" Both. Love unites grace and truth.

GRACE

The parable of the unforgiving servant (Matthew 18:23 – 35) gives a strong warning: beneficiaries of grace should be benefactors of grace. Forgiven leaders should be gracious leaders. Only those Christians whose good works have earned God's favor are exempt from the obligation to lead with grace ... and that would be nobody — except Jesus. Yet he was the most gracious of all. For grace to find its way into our leadership, it needs to find its way into our hearts — from the heart to the thoughts to the actions. Grace travels from inside out.

Beneficiaries of grace should be benefactors of grace. Forgiven leaders should be gracious leaders.

In December of 1990, we decided to drive from our home in Indiana to the Colorado Rockies for a Christmas ski vacation. Scheduled to arrive at my niece's house in Colorado Springs on Christmas Eve, we found ourselves pulling into Denver four hours early, the direct result of my success in convincing our children, much to their mother's fury, that when traveling, things like toilets, restaurants, and beds are luxuries. We would stop for fuel, and nothing else.

With the extra time, I suggested we find a family who couldn't afford Christmas presents and we could be their Santa Claus. We located a wonderful mission where a woman and child had recently walked in, hoping for a Christmas. We met them, got their address, and agreed to see them at their place in two hours.

After the most enjoyable and spirited Christmas shopping we had ever experienced, we headed for the home of this very disadvantaged mother and child. When we arrived at their house, which was a nicer house than I expected, the man who answered the door announced that our friends weren't home. He directed us to put the presents under the tree with "all the rest of the presents." I was flushed with chagrin. We climbed back into the van, and before I could open my angry mouth, ten-year-old Ben began his report to Bonnie: "Mom, the greatest thing happened. Someone must have done the same thing we did and brought them Christmas presents, too."

The leader most of us want to follow is the one who reacts like Ben. Who's to say my cynical response has greater truth value than Ben's gracious assumption? Generally, drawing the negative inference does absolutely no good. Besides denying people the benefit of the doubt, the weeds of anger, frustration, condescension, and other sins begin to choke our spirit. While making unfair attributions to others, we strangle our own hearts.

Good leaders move swiftly, but not so fast as to lose their suspenders. When learning of troubling behavior from someone in their group, they will march toward the problem, but they will suspend their judgment of *why* the behavior is occurring . . . and that's hard to do. As I mentioned in chapter 2, our human tendency is to fill an information vacuum. A famed University of Kansas professor, Fritz Heider, wrote a doctoral dissertation in 1925 that argued all people are innately given to understanding and controlling their environment; hence, we all become "naïve psychologists." From this and subsequent studies, Heider launched what social psychologists now refer to as attribution theory. Essentially, he argued that human beings are wired from birth to question *why* people behave as they do. And if no clear explanation rises to the surface, we humans will make one up. That's not a bad thing, it's just a human thing. But it's a critically important human thing for leaders to understand. People think they know our motives, and we think we know theirs. And sometimes both we and they are wrong.

I once supervised a man who responded to most everything pensively. He greeted all assignments and requests with a slow nod, as though his neck muscles were just starting to thaw. When I realized that was his style, I didn't worry about it. But when I first met him I wondered why he lacked enthusiasm. I tried to peek into the sanctuary of his motives. Was he judging the wisdom of my request? Was he fearful? Was he skeptical? Was he trying to undercut my authority? Did he just not like me? The answer to these "motive" questions affects how we provide leadership. And inquiring minds, as they say, want to know. It helps to know. But beyond people telling us, it's a calculated guess.

Most leaders think about grace as a synonym for kindness in our actions. Grace is certainly that. But grace doesn't stop with our actions; in fact, charitable attributions should precede our actions by warming the assumptions we make about people's motives. At times this kind of charity might feel like we're denying the obvious truth. Yet, giving the benefit of the doubt does not always mean accepting the doubtful. Often grace-filled attributions lead us *to* the truth.

As a young academic dean, I had to tell a faculty member that her coworkers found her very defensive. How do you deliver *that* message? If she defends herself, it proves your point. If she agrees, it proves your point. She can't win. So, in trying to think of some nice way to protect her self-respect, which I feared I might dismantle, I searched for a gracious motive behind her behavior. It was there I stumbled upon the truth. I realized that this woman was the most loyal faculty member in our division, and she fired both barrels at anyone who criticized us or her efforts to make us better. So I sat down with this woman in a different frame of mind than one of simply going about the task of explaining how distasteful people found her defective character. I assumed her defensiveness was out of loyalty rather than weakness. I assumed that she wanted to grow, which in fact she did.

It would be a different world if we all jumped to the conclusion that everyone really does *want* to do the right thing, even the people we need to correct.

RELEASE OF ENERGY

Grace-filled leadership releases not only warmth but also energy into an organizational culture. Energy dissipates in a climate of fear. Mistakes are too costly. As we think about the organizational culture in our ministries and organizations, we need to ask ourselves what kind of climate we're creating.

One hundred years ago, organizations varied in size and substance, but in structure and culture they were all pretty tall and tight. Over the course of the twentieth century, leaders in some of the best companies in the world began to recognize that they had organizational service upside down. Profits were created in the field, not in the corporate headquarters. So the idea of the sales units serving the corporate center had to be flipped. Upper management began to see its central purpose as serving the sales offices and stores, rather than the other way around. It was this recognition that inspired Robert Greenleaf's excellent work on servant leadership. These corporate centers sought to empower rather than control the people in the field. With that empowerment came the unleashing of creativity, energy, and healthy pride.

Whether from a leader or from a corporate center, empowerment without grace turns out to be fake empowerment. "Bob, I've given you the

PREDICTABLE TYPES OF BEHAVIOR

Climate of Grace	Climate of Fear
Risk	Caution
Self-direction	Obedience
Service of mission	Service of leaders
Spontaneous	Secretive
Bold	Tentative

tools, the training, the time, and the authority to tackle this job. Go get 'em, brother. Oh, one more thing, Bob: if you botch this job I will clean out the barrels on you." One of a leader's most empowering tools is truth expressed in a spirit of grace. Grace favors trust over cynicism. Grace corrects kindly, not in a mean-spirited way. Grace celebrates what people do right, while acknowledging honestly where they need to improve. Grace restores confidence. Grace gives energy.

When we lead with grace it sets a cultural tone in our work groups. In my days as a youth director, the dipstick usually came out pretty dry when I measured the grace of various packs of teens. The female venom proved deadlier than what males offered, but I think that was a function of the girls' skill more than the guys' virtue. I would be tempted to offer teens some kind of hormonal exemption from grace were it not for the exceptions we see in those rare grace-filled youth programs.

Our oldest daughter ran for a cross-country team empowered by the fuel of affirmation and grace. I marveled at the coach's relentless charity, even in those rare defeats. When the team finished second in the state meet by a tiny margin, tears flowed. In the post-meet moments with the coach, one of the girls asked what they would have needed to win. Tough spot. One of their best runners had run well below her ability; our daughter Brenna, however, had run the race of her life and every team member knew it. Immediately and compassionately the coach replied, "If somehow Brenna could have picked up just four more places, we'd have made it." In one stroke, he protected the most vulnerable girl by bringing attention to the least vulnerable girl. Coach Wes Player deserved the grace-smart coach of the year award. His players loved him, and they ran fast for him.

Grace never lowers our demands or expectations. In fact, while lifting those we lead, grace also puts leaders in a stronger position to lift expectations. The implicit message of grace is that the leader has confidence—confidence in the resilience, redemption, and strength of the people being led.

It is in offering grace that we discover one of the most reliable and powerful leadership principles: *you get what you give*. When we trust, we are trusted. When we doubt, we are doubted. When we give the benefit of the doubt, we receive the benefit of the doubt. Grace circles back to bless the leader. Over time, being filled with grace fills others with grace.

TRUTH

Sometimes leaders lie. As I mentioned in chapter 2, Sarbanes-Oxley legislation costs U.S. businesses billions of dollars every year, dollars that could go to shareholders, research, charities, or the bottom line. We pay these watchdog dues because business leaders told lies. Obscenely rich people told lies to get richer. Presidents lie too. The president of the United States lied when he denied knowledge of an attempt to cover up the Watergate break-in. Religious leaders lie about money and sex. Athletes lie about steroid use. College presidents lie about SAT scores, endowments, and how much they loved that chicken dinner. Not every leader lies, and not any leader lies about everything; but some leaders have been more filled with spin than filled with truth.

Lying leaders aren't the only problem. Truth has also gotten rather hard to pin down. It isn't quite as cut and dried as it used to be. In some ways, I regret this. I was taught that truth is truth. It still bothers me when people attach modifiers to the word "true." Absolutes need no modifier. Ironically, we often modify absolutes with the word "absolutely." What's the difference between perfect and absolutely perfect? Perfect is perfect. What's the difference between essential and absolutely essential? Essential is essential. So, what do we mean when we use the phrase absolutely true? It's redundant. It is, except in the galaxy of complex issues and situations

Truth slips and slithers in morally weak hands, but it is the scepter of trust in Christlike leadership.

facing today's leaders. While *very* adds no truth value in stating "two plus two equals *very* four," it does add truth value when we honestly confess to a coworker that we are *very* wrong for an insensitivity. Truth comes in all shades and degrees in the real world of leadership. It can be weakened, strengthened, abused, and concealed. Truth slips and slithers in morally weak hands, but it is the scepter of trust in Christlike leadership.

As Christian leaders, we must tell the truth, but we must understand the truth we are telling. Pontius Pilate asked the question we must ask: "What is truth?" In the twenty-first century, this is not a rhetorical question. The answer shouldn't be hard, but it is. It's hard because the way we think about truth changes. When we speak the truth, what do our people hear? I think Christian leaders need to consider truth on three levels: cultural, theological, and personal.

CULTURAL UNDERSTANDING OF TRUTH

A few days ago I went through an intersection that reminded me of a collision. It wasn't a collision between two vehicles; it was a collision between modern and postmodern understandings of truth. Modernism is all about facts. Facts are facts. Postmodernism is all about perception, and perception is biased by our backgrounds. If memory serves me well, with both speed and innocence I bore down on this intersection while traveling a desolate road in the least populated county in the state of Washington. Alas, that day it was neither so desolate nor so underpopulated to exclude a policeman from roaring down the road onto which I must have been anxious to turn. When he pulled me over, he asked if I knew why he stopped me. Passing by all the smart-mouthed replies that entered my head (boredom, needed my advice, wanted to compliment me on the way I controlled my fishtailing after mashing on the brakes when I spotted him, etc.), I said, "You thought I rolled through the stop sign?" Contemptuously, he replied, "No, I didn't *think* you rolled through the stop sign. You did roll through the stop sign." It was then I discovered postmodernism had not quite found its way to Ione, Washington. I thought about helping him see how his *modern* response could be deconstructed by explaining that he was biased by his maleness, his whiteness, his ruralness, and his socially shaped understanding of what it means to stop; but I chose to keep my front teeth instead. Actually, the only thing that kept me from a ticket and maybe even a pistol whipping was that I couldn't keep from laughing at how ridiculous I sounded. Fortunately, it made him laugh too.

In the past one thousand years truth has moved through three (admittedly oversimplified) sea changes. From medieval times through the Renaissance, truth generally referred to revelation authorized by the church. From the Enlightenment into the twentieth century, truth became less faith-connected and more reason-based; science dethroned theology. In the pluralistic twenty-first century, truth gets defined, if not created, by culture and social context. Shifting its loyalty from the church, to science, and now to culture, "truth" has moved like a flat-footed matador — slowly, but elusively.

In the first half of the last millennium, truth was protected and defined by the church. Truth always carried a theological overtone. It also carried some heavy artillery and was used by Christians in ways that are disturbingly similar to how it is now used by Muslim terrorists. In the medieval and pre-Renaissance times, faith, politics, and culture were far more integrated than in subsequent periods, and faith carried the most weight.

Next came the Enlightenment thinkers of the eighteenth and nineteenth centuries who elbowed aside all things mystical and sat down in the seat of reason and science. Theology, once considered the queen of the sciences, became superfluous if not threatening to the galloping god of objectivity. Truth in this new world of science required the kind of empirical properties that transcendence by its very definition could never provide. Left in the dust were the residual influences of religion that provided at least modest inventories of moral capital for Enlightenment thinkers. At the very beginning of the Enlightenment, French philosopher Blaise Pascal sounded the warning that science alone leaves us wanting and vulnerable. "Physical science will not console me for the ignorance of morality in the time of affliction. But the science of ethics will always console me for the ignorance of the physical sciences" (*Pensees* #67, 1656).

Today we find ourselves in what academics label as a postmodern or post-Enlightenment world. Absolute truth has been unseated by relative, culture-shaped truth. Subjectivity has arraigned objectivity on charges of being unknowable, unprovable, and certainly unfashionable. The postmodern answer to Pilate's question "What is truth?" comes in the form of a question, "Whose truth?" Even scientific and mathematical areas that once occupied the safety zones of "objective truth" no longer enjoy the status of certainty. This notion of truth barks worse than it bites for those of us who follow Christ. Yesterday's modernists had no trouble with objective truth, but matters of faith were dismissed as subjective, unprovable. Today's postmodernists are fine with the subjectivity of faith and spirituality but they want to strip out any ideas about absolute truth.

This is all rather academic until a young professional objects to your claim that Jesus is the only way to salvation. The postmodern response to your claim is very different from the modern response and illustrates how these two philosophies land differently in the streets and in the pews. Today's postmodern yuppie replies, "Jesus is *your* truth and *your* way to salvation." Yesterday's modern yuppie would shoot back with "Prove it!" The good news of postmodernism is that our faith has become respectable; the bad news is that the idea of universal truth has become unrespectable. Postmodern thinking has allowed faith to reach culture more broadly but with less depth. It's easier to talk about faith and spirituality, but when we drill down to the objective truth of our faith we encounter more resistance. Catholic priest and noted author Richard Neuhaus laments:

> Clear thinking about moral truth founders on the rocks of relativism and subjectivism. In a radically individualistic culture, we do not

> discern and obey what is objectively true. Rather, each of us decides what is "true for me." We *create* the truth. This, however, is really not so new, according to the Pope. It is a way of thinking and acting that began with that unfortunate afternoon in the Garden of Eden and has resulted in herds of independent minds marching toward moral oblivion with Mr. Sinatra's witless boast on their lips, "I did it my way." The "postmodernist" twist on this is to argue that all morality is created by culture. We are socially constructed, it is said, "all the way down." (*First Things*, January 1994, vol. 40, pp. 14–29)

This is our leadership playing field. So, how do we lead in a Christlike way on such slippery ground? Before suggesting a few answers to that question, two other perspectives on truth bear mentioning.

THEOLOGICAL UNDERSTANDING OF TRUTH

Truth is Jesus Christ—the way, the truth, and the life. Everything a Christian leader looks at should come under the illumination of Christ's light. When we reverse that and see Jesus in light of profit, popularity, productivity, or any other leadership value, we can still be Christians who lead, but we stop being Christlike leaders.

In October 1993, Pope John Paul II issued his tenth encyclical, *Veritatis Splendor* (The Splendor of Truth). In this masterful examination of truth in the world, the pope hailed the elevated importance of freedom as expressed in the fall of the Berlin Wall and the breakup of the Soviet Union. But freedom, the pope argued, cannot stand alone without collapsing into a kind of license that ends up denying freedom. "Freedom must be ordered to truth." Truth, with all of its moral expressions, forms the backbone of freedom. Moral relativism turns out to be an anarchist in a liberator's clothing.

As Christians we believe in absolutes. Early church councils affirmed the anchors of our faith. Jesus made absolute claims. He said he is the only way to God—a rather incendiary remark in today's pluralistic world. But as Christian leaders our stout defenses against attacks on moral and spiritual absolutes often omit the way in which we embrace these absolutes—by faith. As finite creatures, we cannot know absolutes absolutely. When Jesus claims to be the only way to the Father, by faith we believe him. It is not an absolute claim that we mortals can prove empirically. But evidence supporting the reliability of Scripture, along with witnessing the profound impact of Christ's transforming love, allows us to hold a reason-based faith that Jesus was telling the truth.

Earlier I observed that postmodernism trips over itself when it attempts to discredit religious faith. But the faith of postmodernism is just the opposite of faith in God. Postmodernists believe in subjective truth absolutely, while Christians believe in absolute truth subjectively. Biblical faith is subjective in that it rests on trust and evidence, not on empirical proof. Terms such as "hope," "expectation," "assurance," "confidence," and even "faith" all have the ring of the apostle Paul's admission that we see through a glass dimly. Because ultimately faith finds occupancy in the heart and mind of the subject, it admits to being subjective and can't honestly be assailed by postmodern arguments. Biblical faith is a blessed hope we cradle and embrace, not an empirical fact we prove and wield.

Biblical faith is a blessed hope we cradle and embrace, not an empirical fact we prove and wield.

As Christian leaders, our theology of truth should divide itself into what we believe and how we believe it. In the world of philosophy we call this ontology (the study of what is true) and epistemology (the study of how we come to know what is true). Ontologically, orthodox Christianity affirms God's truth as absolute, uncompromising, unchangeable, and unaffected by human opinion or response. Truth is Jesus Christ from age to age. It is revealed in Christ, in Holy Scripture, and in the glory of God's creation. Epistemologically, however, we hold these absolute truths *by faith*, faith that sees through a glass darkly until that day of consummate truth when we stand face-to-face with Christ. It is out of this theology of truth we assemble our personal commitment to truth.

PERSONAL UNDERSTANDING OF TRUTH

On June 12, 1964, the falsehood of apartheid handed Nelson Mandela a term of life imprisonment in the Union of South Africa. His only hope was truth. After twenty-six years of incarceration and the efforts of many, truth set Mandela free.

President F. W. de Klerk and Mandela reached an agreement, and on February 2, 1990, apartheid was formally lifted. Now, their nation was faced with the question of how to restore justice. Reconciliation without justice leaves a mountain under the rug where hurt and wrong and truth have been swept. Should these crimes against humanity be settled in the retributive justice of Nuremberg-type tribunals? Nelson Mandela and Bishop Desmond Tutu had fought for truth, sacrificed for truth, and been freed by truth. They knew revenge was incomplete justice, incomplete truth. Restoration for a crime against humanity must restore humanity, not just those directly victimized. So in an astonishing act of grace and unflinching commitment to the truth, they created the Truth and Reconciliation Commission. All those who would come forward and confess fully the truth of their apartheid crimes would be granted amnesty. In modern times, this was truth's most powerful hour.

At a very personal level, great leaders are truthful leaders. They demand it from themselves and from those who follow them. Great leaders are honest, just, realistic, optimistic, enduring, reconciling, responsible, and empowering. Truth demands honesty. Truth demands realism. Truth demands justice. Truth offers hope. Truth endures. Truth reconciles. Truth requires acceptance of responsibility. Truth liberates.

What does a commitment to truth look like when fostered by a leader of ordinary station working toward a goal not quite as lofty as the freedom of a nation? What does it look like if you're chief of the parts department rather than chief of state, if you're a pastor, if you're a teacher, if you're a small group leader? Frankly, a commitment to truth doesn't really change with the stakes. You need to *hear* the truth. And you need to *tell* the truth.

Hearing the Truth

America got pounded by Hurricane Katrina, its greatest natural disaster in the past century. Perhaps our lack of preparedness can be forgiven, but the clumsiness of our response cannot. Some feel this cataclysmic event exposed in President Bush the kind of repulsion of dissent that historian Arthur Schlesinger found in John F. Kennedy's presidency. *Newsweek*'s Evan Thomas wrote:

> [President] Bush can be petulant about dissent; he equates disagreement with disloyalty. After five years in office, he is surrounded largely by people who agree with him. Bush can ask tough questions, but it's mostly a one-way street.... Most presidents keep a devil's advocate around. When Hurricane Katrina struck, it appears there was no one to tell President Bush the plain truth: that the state and local governments had been overwhelmed.... ("How Bush Blew It," *Newsweek*, September 19, 2005)

Whether or not this analysis is fully accurate, it does make the point that a commitment to truth requires a leader to keep truth channels open. Warren Bennis observes, "What makes a good follower? The single most important characteristic may well be a willingness to tell the truth. In a world of growing complexity leaders are increasingly dependent on their subordinates for good information, whether the leaders want to hear it or not. Followers who tell the truth and leaders who listen to it are an unbeatable combination." (*Managing the Dream: Reflections on Leadership and Change* [Perseus Publishing, 2000], p. 269)

A faculty member stopped by my office a couple of years ago to discuss a few operational issues. At one point, he looked at me and said, "You're really liked around here." (Now here's a discerning person, I thought.) "But does anyone ever tell you when you're full of crap?" Good for him. It's an important question for any leader. Leaders committed to truth must welcome stressful information and create climates of safety for providing it.

Commitment to the truth means listening with discernment. Leaders do not honor truth by giving unexamined acceptance to all prophets. One of our faculty leaders introduces every concern with, "I'm hearing ..." and never with "I feel...." This kind of vague framing makes it difficult for me to grasp the magnitude or breadth of the concern. Nurturing truth does not mean accepting everything you hear without probing and verifying.

Finally, leaders need to hear the truth while protecting themselves from debilitating truth tellers. Chronic criticism or alarm will destroy our ability to discriminate truth from general pessimism. When "wolf, wolf" applies to everything, it doesn't apply to anything. Our source loses credibility and we are left in charge of deciding if there really is a wolf. That can be hard to do, especially if I'm the wolf.

I think most leaders suffer from hearing too little rather than too much truth. It is worth asking:

- Who is my most reliable truth teller?
- Do I need to create a warmer climate for truth telling?
- Do I ever get defensive when I hear the truth? Am I sending mixed messages about how much truth I really want?

TELLING THE TRUTH

Christian leaders bear duty to tell three kinds of truth—hard truth, plain truth, and God's truth.

Hard truth. Many of us cower from those occasions calling us to deliver hard truth. But sometimes to keep silent is to lie, deceive, or fail to warn. G. K. Chesterton once said, "If something's worth doing, it's worth doing badly." If you need to say you're sorry, it's better to stumble through a poorly expressed apology than remain silent because you don't know what to say. Chesterton's aphorism applies to telling the truth, but Christian leaders don't have to tell the truth badly. We are children of grace. We can speak the truth in love.

One truth-protecting benefit of grace accrues not only to the listener, but also to the one speaking the truth. As I indicated earlier, truth without grace arouses defensiveness. But grace calms, and in my experience it calms both the sender and the receiver. Research in the area of cognitive complexity (a person's ability to form impressions that have both favorable and unfavorable aspects) suggests that high levels of emotion cloud our ability to see the nuances and complexities of a situation (so love *really is* rather blind). Our impressions become grossly positive or negative. We find it difficult to take angular points of view. Our analytical tools dull into blunt objects. We reduce the complex into the simple. G. K. Chesterton also said, "For every complex problem there is a simple solution; and it's wrong." Grace opens our eyes to complexity.

Telling the truth in love helps evacuate anger and defensiveness from a situation. Often it will convert the atmosphere of a conversation from telling to interacting, from punishing to advising, from declaring to probing. Gracious truth telling can mean taking responsibility for how you felt when your subordinate responded to one of your ideas by labeling it "not very wise." To say gracelessly, "You made me look dumb when you tried to undercut me," imputes a motive and abdicates responsibility for your feelings. A more exploratory discussion will follow an observation such as, "Your remark felt a bit personal to me. Tell me more about what you meant by your reaction to my idea."

Plain truth. A commitment to truth requires aggressive honesty. As I said in chapter 2, openness hangs a cupola of accountability over everything we do and all the ways we lead. Truth and accountability are close friends. But accountability does a better job of preventing falsehood than promoting truth.

In the fall of 1996 we experienced a significant drop in the percentage of accepted students who ended up enrolling. Because we enjoyed a spike in our retention rate, the budget worked. But that spring we had to establish salary increases for the following year. All of our enrollment data looked good, but "no shows" were unpredictable. So, violating my stated goal to increase salaries aggressively for seven consecutive years, I recommended a modest increase. I just didn't know if the drop in our yield rate was an aberration or the beginning of a trend. In God's good grace, the 1996 yield turned out to be only a one-year downward blip, and we broke an enrollment record in the fall of 1997.

In truth, we would have given bigger raises had we known our freshman enrollment would bounce back. In truth, we lost our nerve (although responsibly, I felt). In truth, we started the 1997 year with money in the jar that we would have given to our very effective and hardworking people "if we knew then what we know now." So at the end of September, we gave everyone a check for five hundred dollars at a total cost of $170,000. We asked folks not to thank us because, in truth, it was our mistake in the first place. And the last morsel of painful truth is that our employees still suffer from that mistake because the five hundred dollars didn't go to their base salaries that get increased annually on a percentage basis.

We goofed. But the good thing about this story is that we were motivated by truth. Because this doesn't always happen in our industry, we did get thanked and it probably raised folks' trust in the administration. But that shouldn't really matter. We're Christians. Being truthful is what matters.

Leaders would do well to talk with their work groups about committing to truth. Truth competes with spin, with internal and external pressures, and it even clashes with the noble goals of our organizations. I'm halfway through Jonathan Aitken's book on Chuck Colson (*Charles*

W. Colson: A Life Redeemed [Doubleday, 2005]). That Richard Nixon loved his country cannot be contested. That telling the truth ranked way below his love of country is also incontestable. We need a mentality from which we look at situations, information, and people with the recognition that to lead in the name of Jesus Christ means leading in the name of grace and truth.

God's truth. Telling God's truth is different than telling painful truth or plain truth, even though it can include both. I can best introduce what I mean with the words of Vaclav Havel, one of the great political truth tellers of the twentieth century. At the University of Michigan's spring 2000 commencement he said:

> But what is truth? It is of paramount importance to understand the fine difference between information and truth.
>
> To put it briefly and simply, I believe that truth is information but, at the same time, it is something greater. Truth—like any other information—is information which has been clearly proved, or affirmed, or verified within a certain system of coordinates or paradigms, or which is simply convincing. But it is more than that—it is information avouched by a human being with his or her whole existence, with his or her reputation and name, with his or her honor.... Truth means standing firm no matter whether it yields returns or not, whether it meets with universal recognition or universal condemnation, whether a fight for truth leads to success or to absolute scorn and to obscurity.

As Christian leaders, if we are filled with God's truth, it will show. If we have avouched God's truth with our whole existence, name, and honor, it will show. If we stand willing to fight for God's truth even if it leads to absolute scorn and obscurity, it will show.

I believe we have entered an age in which Christian leaders should get faith back out on their shirtsleeves. I've only heard "Harry doesn't wear his faith on his shirtsleeve" as a compliment. Why doesn't Harry want faith on his shirtsleeve? I don't think it stains. I'd like to hear someone lament, "Poor Harry, he can't seem to get his faith out there on his shirtsleeve."

I believe we have entered an age in which Christian leaders should get faith back out on their shirtsleeves.

I'm worse than Harry at letting God's truth show. My only qualification for even commenting on this is that I'm better than I used to be. A thin credential, I admit. Some Christian leaders reflect God's truth warmly and compellingly. For example, you can't know Dr. Earl Palmer, pastor emeritus of University Presbyterian Church in Seattle, and not know how much he loves literature and art. By shining the illuminating light of faith on this love, God's truth gets reflected in Earl's teaching, preaching, and ordinary conversation. We would do well to allow the passions of our own lives to serve as portals for Christ's light to shine.

There are very identifiable reasons for the virtual invisibility of God's truth in the work and lives of Christian leaders. Reckoning with these influences helps position us for new opportunities to show God's truth in our leadership.

- *Culture.* The twentieth-century exaltation of science and technology discouraged us from making explicit the influence of faith on our leadership. It felt soft. And that feeling is hard to shake off.
- *Denominational effects.* Mainline Protestant denominations tend to treat faith as a private matter. Members are better at reciting the creeds than at giving their testimonies. The Roman Catholic Church treated faith as deeply ecclesial. Members were urged to embrace church dogma rather than improvise faith. Both influences reinforced any personal timidity a leader would have in discussing matters of faith.
- *Evangelical influences.* Many evangelicals never learned to live out faith naturally. When our churches tried to talk us into seeing all

> exchanges with non-Christians as evangelistic opportunities, we took on ulterior motives, became too strategic, and lost our spontaneity. References to faith assumed preachy or evangelistic tones that made many of us uncomfortable or proud or both.

I've had several watershed experiences prompt me to think about integrating my faith openly and naturally into life and leadership. I've searched for the sweet spot between spiritualizing and silence. I've erred toward the latter. But sometimes relationships drew from me very natural expressions of faith. I recall one night after a park district basketball game our team ended up at the local tavern. Somehow I made reference to a visit my kids and I had taken earlier in the week to a women's shelter. The ensuing questions moved from predictably irreverent to sincere. After they got the women's shelter wisecracks out of their system, they asked what I was doing there.

"Taking Christmas presents."

"How many?"

"Sixty."

"Why?"

And I just told them. "God has been so good to us — it makes my family happy, it makes the women happy, and I suspect it makes God happy." They absolutely loved it. A faith-inspired act impressed them far more than if I had hit a last-second shot to win our game, which I didn't.

This incident took place in a bar twenty-five years ago. Since then, I've assumed that I could express Christ openly anywhere that isn't less conducive to faith ... which is everywhere. I've also been on alert for moments when my expressions could be authentic and not forced.

Now I work in a Christian organization. I probably get points for doing what Christian leaders in secular organizations can do only with great circumspection. But I still fail too often to make the living Christ a living part of my leadership. The acid test for us Christian leaders is when and where the truth of Christ shows. We should add to the old question,

"If you were accused of being a Christian would there be enough evidence to convict you?" another question, "Where would someone have to look to find evidence?" The answer should be "anywhere." We need to be reflectors of Christ's truth as well as his light.

Those of us who lead Christian organizations need to develop and activate a philosophy and strategy for the open integration of God's truth with our leadership. Our habits, our culture, and our organizations encourage us to segregate our faith from our leadership. If we say with the Heidelberg Catechism that our lives are not our own, we ought to find integrating faith and leadership quite natural. But we should never stop asking the questions: "How is my leadership reflecting my commitment to Christ?" "Does it show?" "If it does show, how would anyone know that Christ is what's showing?"

It is at this point I find the influence of postmodern thinking an ally rather than an enemy. No matter what kind of group we lead or the environment in which we lead it, we can take advantage of the twenty-first century's acceptance of all things spiritual. Drawing a bold line between modernism and postmodernism is ridiculous. Living can't happen without acknowledging the powerful presence of modernism's objectivity and postmodernism's subjectivity. But the climate to refer openly to matters of faith has definitely warmed up. Earlier this morning, I saw a press release from the Atlanta Braves that today is another "Faith Days with the Braves." After the game tonight contemporary Christian singer Jeremy Camp will do a concert for all who wish to stay. The event will also include a testimony by a former Braves player. For those of you who are keeping score at home, mark this down as unbelievable! We can cry all we want about culture being more permissive, MTV, and gay marriage, but culture is also permitting expressions of faith we never could have imagined. So we shouldn't waste energy whining about how bad things are when we could be taking advantage of an opportunity to proclaim the risen and living Christ.

LEADING WITH GRACE AND TRUTH

We pick and choose how we want to be like Jesus. But mostly we want Jesus to be like us. It has been said that God created us in his own image; then we returned the favor. So when we get angry, we point to the cleansing of the temple. When we get soft, we point to the "seventy times seven" forgiveness quotient. We prefer not to look at Jesus holistically. We can be like Jesus and get upset. We can be like Jesus and get sentimental. But we cannot be like Jesus without being filled with grace and truth.

Christlike leaders will look at every situation and ask two questions: *What is the grace-filled thing to do? What is the truth-filled thing to do?* Rarely will the answers conflict. Grace leads to truth and truth leads to grace. When we dismiss a person for the right reasons, we are telling the truth, truth that can graciously enlighten a person and lead to growth. And when we give "one more chance" for the right reasons, we are extending grace, grace that can awaken the truth that the person does have the gifts and abilities to succeed in the job. But in those rare times when we just can't find a way to reconcile grace and truth, let's choose grace. God did.

The consummation of Christ "leading from the middle of his people" was his dying in the middle of two thieves. On that Easter weekend, Jesus the leader became Jesus our Savior. Leadership based on God's incarnation cannot ignore the ultimate act of grace—the cross. Our sacrifices in the name of grace—looking weak, risking failure, moving too slowly, being wrong—are trivial compared to Christ's gracious sacrifice. But we must be willing to make them. Bridging the gap can demand time, energy, access, emotional involvement, and often the forfeiture of some "right." For Jesus, dwelling among his people in grace and truth cost him everything, but it made him the greatest leader who ever lived. It made him our Savior.

QUESTIONS FOR REFLECTION AND DISCUSSION

1. Think back on an occasion when a leader confronted you about a performance issue. Did you feel threatened or empowered? What was it about the manner in which you were confronted that made you feel the way you did?
2. The author states that most of the time your associates want to do the right thing. Do you agree? Try to recall an incident when an associate "blew it." What might have been the "good motives" that led to his or her mistake?
3. What does the author mean when he says, "Truth comes in all shades and degrees in the real world of leadership"? In your own world of leadership, have you ever been tempted to "shade the truth"? Explain. Could grace have been applied to that situation?
4. How has society's suspicion of "absolutes" affected the way you minister to your people? How has it affected the way you work with your associates? Do you view the influence of postmodernism as a threat or an ally? Why?
5. Your church or organization is struggling financially and you have to deliver the news that salaries will be frozen and certain benefits reduced. What role can grace play as you tell these truths to your subordinates? How can grace make you a better leader when your ministry struggles?

5

Sacrificing

Who, being in very nature God,
did not consider equality with God something to be grasped,
but made himself nothing,
taking the very nature of a servant,
being made in human likeness.
And being found in appearance as a man,
he humbled himself
and became obedient to death — even death on a cross!

Philippians 2:6 – 8

On June 28, 2005, Lieutenant Michael Murphy and three other Navy Seals found themselves under attack by more than fifty Taliban fighters in Afghanistan. Needing a more open space to transmit a call for assistance, Murphy crawled into a certain line of fire and sent the message. It cost him his life. Upon receiving the Medal of Honor for their son's sacrifice, Murphy's parents characterized his actions not as those of a hero, but those of a leader.

In one act of obedience, Jesus raised the stakes for any of us who really dare to follow his example as a leader: he laid his life down for his followers.

For the incarnation of God to have any bearing on our understanding of leadership, sacrifice is inescapable. Paul's letter to the Philippian church traces Christ's incarnate path — from humility to service to sacrifice. Christ came not to be served but to serve, to give his life as a ransom for many.

Being a leader doesn't necessarily mean losing your life, but being a Christlike leader does mean sacrifice. It has to. Sacrifice stands as the alpha and omega of the incarnation. Leaving a throne for a manger, leaving a king's life for a nomadic life, and then consummating those departures for the most ignominious of all deaths means we cannot avoid sacrifice if we hope to lead like Jesus.

What is sacrifice? We probably throw the term around rather loosely. It seems to me that for an act to qualify as a sacrifice, big or small, it requires a denial of self in service of other people and high purposes. Often the impact exceeds the magnitude of the sacrifice. One of the most powerful demonstrations of sacrifice in my life came from my father as he sat like a bump on a log, motionless and bored.

It was our summer vacation, the same summer vacation we had every year. We drove six hundred miles to my grandparents', spent a week chatting, and then headed back home. That was the drill, except on one anomalous night when my father took me to some kind of a car race near my grandparents' town. At some point he must have given me money to get a treat, or maybe I had to go to the bathroom. The former would have been rare for my dad, but no eleven-year-old boy has ever had to go to the bathroom during an auto race, so it must have been the treat. As I was walking back toward the stands, I spotted my dad, frozen faced, just sitting there by himself. And for reasons I still don't fully understand, I stopped and stared. I was utterly overcome. At that moment, I realized my dad didn't really care about the race. He sat there for one reason and one reason alone. He sat there because he loved me. I don't care how little he had to sacrifice for that one evening. Who knows, maybe he needed as much of a break from chatting with Grandma as I did. That didn't matter. In my mind, he sacrificed an evening to be with me, his son. He gave up something to give me worth. And I am still warmed by this memory of gazing at my father for what could not have been more than five seconds.

Sacrifices great and small contrast sharply with the shameless self-interest that grips twenty-first century America. Marketers have followed, or perhaps led the shift. Sales pitches have moved from "Wouldn't you *like* this credit card you can use anywhere in the world?" to "You really *need* this credit card for any kind of a life" to "You so *deserve* this passport to happiness." Deserve? No you don't. What did you do to deserve it? And how does some guy writing a commercial know what you deserve? "Deserve" language appeals nakedly to our self-aggrandizement, and it must work or they wouldn't use it.

But just as we are about to drown in self-absorption, the nobility of someone's simple sacrifice rescues us. "You look like you're in a hurry, please go ahead of me." "Why don't I take the middle seat so you two can sit together?" "Let me watch your kids tonight; it's been way too long since you've been out." We see the despair in serving only ourselves. We see valor in those who consider others above themselves. We see grace ripple across the lives of those for whom sacrifices are offered. We see sacrifice beget sacrifice. We see a better way. We see the scarred hands of Christ.

Sacrifices inspire us and lead us. What leaders shrug their shoulders at opportunities to inspire? Even trivial sacrifices can motivate those we lead. I sacrifice two or three hours a year darting around like a drunken sailor grabbing every piece of litter I see as I walk across campus. On the clock, it would make more sense for me to walk in straight lines and have a lesser paid person worry about the trash. But I'm setting an example, presumably inspiring those in our community to join the litter detail. In the long haul, my "sacrifice" saves the university money if picking up litter becomes a campus value. Sacrifices generally inspire, but inspiration isn't the only reason or the highest reason to sacrifice. If it were, then we would always need to make sacrifices visible. Their value would be primarily symbolic, performed for the instrumental purposes of inspiring our people and authenticating our leadership. Inspiration and authentication are vitally important and inextricably linked. But they enjoy their greatest impact as by-products of a higher purpose for making sacrifices.

The most powerful reason to sacrifice is the one that sent Christ to the cross. We sacrifice for the mission, for the people executing the mission, and for the people served by the mission. It begs the definition of "sacrifice" if we give something up only to strengthen our position or deepen our influence. Between the high and low extremes of dying for our country and picking up litter we make sacrifices that are inspired by our mission and our love for the people involved in that mission. If these people are inspired, that's great; and if our leadership becomes more validated, that's great too. But we sacrifice largely because we have subordinated our self-interests to our mission and our people.

It begs the definition of "sacrifice" if we give something up only to strengthen our position or deepen our influence.

I have a friend named Jeff Kemp who got banged around as a quarterback in the National Football League for more than ten years. He tells a wonderful story of how the legendary coach, Bill Walsh, taught sacrifice to the San Francisco 49ers:

> My favorite play was a play-action pass to Jerry Rice, "Brown Right, Fake 22, Z Post." The line was to dive left and cut block as they would on a running play. The halfback was to explode up and over the line, wrapping up an imaginary ball, as he, like the linemen, sacrificed himself to convince the defense of a run play. The wide

> receivers briefly feign run blocking until Rice would dash past his coverage cornerback and behind a run-suspecting, flat-footed free safety.
>
> The quarterback was to turn from the defense, fake a handoff, and watch the running back like a matador following a bull ... then, swiftly set up to pass a long post route,... caught [by Rice] approaching the end zone, just after the quarterback [was] driven into the ground by the defensive end who had to go unblocked in order to sell the fake run. "It's a price we pay for a big play," Bill confidently predicted. (NFL.com, August 9, 2007)

Although the quarterback gets the MVP ("most *vulnerable* player") award in this story—getting smeared for the sake of freeing the receiver—many of the players had to sacrifice. Sacrifice is not just a duty of our leaders; it offers a means by which everyone can lead. Any sacrifice made in service of the mission, no matter who in the organization makes it, provides leadership for the whole group. Leadership guru Bernard Bass observes that "transforming leadership elevates the importance of the task and inspires followers to put the group interests before their own" (quoted in Gary Yukl, *Leadership in Organizations* [Prentice Hall, 1997], p. 351). It is in this sacrifice of self-interest that leadership ripples through an organization. James MacGregor Burns, in his tour de force entitled *Leadership*, says that transforming leadership is a "relationship of mutual stimulation and elevation that converts followers into leaders and may convert leaders into moral agents" ([HarperCollins, 1978], p. 4). Leadership that instills sacrifice into the organizational culture inspires every member to do what is best for the common good.

One of the most celebrated examples of how a leader's sacrifice converted followers into leaders can be found in the amazing story of Aaron Feuerstein. On December 11, 1995, the Malden Mills textile factory in Lowell, Massachusetts, went up in smoke, a total loss, leaving Feuerstein, the owner, with two good options. In his early seventies, nobody would have blamed him for pocketing the $300 million in insurance money and putting his feet up. And, if he didn't want the sedentary life of retirement, he could have taken this opportunity to reinvest his cash in an offshore manufacturing operation. New England wages were among the highest in the world, and his trademark Polartec fleeces could have been made anywhere. So which option did he choose? Neither. Instead he announced plans to rebuild the plant and pledged that he would keep all employees on the payroll during the reconstruction. He continued paying them for ninety days at a cost of $1.5 million per week while the factories were being rebuilt. He also gave generously to support charities that helped the families of nine critically injured workers who did recover.

Feuerstein was bad at arithmetic if he didn't know how much more this plan would cost than his insurance settlement, but apparently he used a different bottom line than the one below the numbers. He told *Parade* magazine:

> I have a responsibility to the worker, both blue-collar and white-collar. I have an equal responsibility to the community. It would have been unconscionable to put 3,000 people on the streets and deliver a deathblow to the cities of Lawrence and Methuen. Maybe on paper our company is worthless to Wall Street, but I can tell you it's worth more. (March 28, 1996)

A devout Jew, Feuerstein explained his motivation in accepting the Lincoln Award for Ethics and Excellence in Business, sponsored by The Economic Club of Phoenix. Quoting from Jeremiah 9:23–24 in perfect Hebrew, then giving the English translation, his message was, "Let the rich man not praise himself, but rather, by demonstrating the will of God, show kindness, justice, and righteousness in his actions."

The circling conclusion to this story illustrates how this sacrifice created a culture of leadership throughout the company. Several years after the fire and reconstruction, Feuerstein's benevolence caught up with him. His sacrificial efforts ended in bankruptcy. But this time his employees announced that *they* would make the sacrifices. They passed on overtime, accepted lower wages, and stepped up their productivity. In October 2003, Malden Mills emerged from bankruptcy and thrives today.

Sacrifice emerges from the subordination of our self-interest to the mission, to the people who execute the mission, and to the people served by the mission. Aaron Feuerstein wins the trifecta. He deserves all the props and fame he received. But his story climbed the visibility ladder largely on the strength of its scale. How many of us lay awake nights trying to figure out what to do with $300 million? The question for us little guys is whether our puny sacrifices matter. I think they do. They matter to God and they matter to our people.

In 1859 Charles Spurgeon declared it a slander to Christ if we preach anything other than Christ crucified ("The Crisis of This World" in *The Passion and Death of Our Lord*, vol. 6 of *A Treasury of Spurgeon on the Life and Work of Our Lord* [Baker, 1979], p. 8). Sacrifice matters to God. It is the height and depth of the incarnation. It is God's ransom for getting back what sin kidnapped. For us, Christ's sacrificial death and resurrection reign as the best news of the good news. For God, Christ's sacrifice is the worst news, the abject horror that makes the good news possible. Sacrifice matters to God. But Spurgeon went on to say, "There are a few men who scoff at the statement and reject the thought of sacrifice" ("Our Suffering Substitute" in *New Park Street Pulpit* [Pilgrim,1859], pp. 2, 3). Spurgeon stands on the importance of sacrifice to God, but he also acknowledges the enormous power sacrifice has on those who witness it. He argues for its centrality in evangelism. Sacrifice sticks out as active grace that cannot be ignored.

Every sacrifice is local. No book can anticipate the situational factors that determine what opportunities are appropriate for the gift of sacrifice. However, the following categories suggest some of the areas where sacrifice often makes the biggest impact.

SACRIFICING TIME

I will never forget walking past the president's office in my first real job. "Hey, Bill," he called as he was speaking in the outer office with his assistant. "Do you have time to come in and chat for a minute?" Think about that: a guy whose obese schedule I now understand asking me if *I* have time to visit. I was floored. I'm sure I smiled the entire ten minutes we talked. We didn't get much done in that short time, which was pretty much the point, but I never stopped being influenced and energized by those few minutes. For most leaders, decisions about how they spend their time determine their levels of success. Time is precious. And that is what makes the sacrifice of time so jolting. A leader's unrequired presence dissolves the cynicism of even the most jaded people, and it rewards and inspires those who are already anxious to follow.

Leaders generally have less discretionary time than most people, but that scarcity enables them to make an impact with even small sacrifices of time. People appreciate so deeply the attention, support, and accessibility produced by even these modest gestures. While the Whitworth board chair Chuck Boppell was CEO of the company that owns Sizzler steakhouses, he offered to take the day off and help me serve hot dogs at a picnic for family and friends. I couldn't believe it. He was swamped, successfully reversing the fortunes of a company that had been swimming in red ink. But on one Thursday, he left his steaks for my hot dogs . . . and he gave me an image I will never forget.

SACRIFICING COMFORT

Working with college students revokes one of my First Amendment free speech rights. I cannot whine about America's deterioration. I work with an avalanche of evidence to the contrary. I make it a point to eat several meals a week with whatever students happen to be scattered in our dining commons. Even if they represent a fraction of the general population, their everyday commitments to serving others deepens my belief that if somehow my generation can hold this planet together, today's youth will know what to do with it when they get it. Life is good for these future leaders, but the goodness of their lives does raise a concern. It raises a concern about them and about us. Maybe life has gotten a little too good. We like President John Kennedy's question, "Ask not what your country can do for you; ask what you can do for your country." Most of us are willing to help out disadvantaged neighborhoods. But we would like to be able to get to those neighborhoods without crossing our comfort border.

THE CALL TO SACRIFICE

Sacrifice is never easy, so when you feel you have already sacrificed enough for your mission, consider these encouragements:

Greater love has no one than this, that he lay down his life for his friends.

John 15:13

An action of small value performed with much love of God is far more excellent than one of a higher virtue, done with less love of God.

Henry Ward Beecher

Only a life lived for others is worth living.

Albert Einstein

There's only one effectively redemptive sacrifice, the sacrifice of self-will to make room for the knowledge of God.

Aldous Huxley

Love always involves responsibility, and love always involves sacrifice. And we do not really love Christ unless we are prepared to face His task and take up His cross.

William Barclay

In his famed 1899 speech to the Hamilton Club of Chicago, Teddy Roosevelt began, "I wish to preach, not the doctrine of ignoble ease, but the doctrine of the strenuous life, the life of toil and effort, of labor and strife; to preach that highest form of success which comes, not to the man who desires mere easy peace, but to the man who does not shrink from danger, from hardship, or from bitter toil, and who out of these wins the splendid ultimate triumph." Huh? That isn't exactly a twenty-first-century campaign platform. "If you want toil and strife, vote for me." Today's political leaders have made comfort the value proposition of their appeals for support. They claim we're in a war on terrorism but insist we can and should cut taxes. This doesn't jibe with the stories my parents told about national sacrifices made during World War II. Now sacrificing comfort feels, well, un-American, by golly. And contrasting with the daily additions to what we deem entitlements, we hear Emily Elliot's unsettling account of Christ's nativity comforts:

> Thou didst leave Thy throne and Thy kingly crown,
> When Thou camest to earth for me;
> But in Bethlehem's home was there found no room
> For Thy holy nativity.

The magnitude of Christ sacrificing his life overshadows the fact that he also sacrificed countless comforts of life. According to Matthew 8:19, a teacher of the law claimed, "Lord, I will follow you wherever you go." Hmmm. Not so fast, Scribe Man. "Foxes have holes and birds of the air have nests, but the Son of Man has no place to lay his head," Jesus replied. Leaders need to differentiate between provisions that improve their job performance and perquisites that simply make life more comfortable. The former are legitimate; the latter are hard to justify. In my first college presidency, parking was at a premium and I had a reserved spot right across the street from my office. In the presidency I now occupy we have plenty of parking and the best spots get taken in the order of when people come to work. Before, my reserved spot was a huge time-saver, but for me to have one now would be based purely on rank, not need.

I probably make too big of a deal out of comfort sacrifices. They're easy to make and maybe no one notices. But I'm pretty sure that a twenty-first-century Jesus would fly economy class, have a reasonable-sized office, stay at Holiday Inn Express (if not in the parking lot), buy his sandals at Sears unless there was a great sale at Nordstrom, walk or take the bus to work, and order the second least expensive wine, assuming he didn't just order water and "fix" it.

SACRIFICING CREDIT

Author Gus Lee has written a great book on the courage required in providing good leadership (*Courage: The Backbone of Leadership*, [Jossey-Bass, 2006]). I had a chance to ask Gus to identify a couple of his favorite leaders, choosing from the vast number he has watched and advised. The first one he mentioned was Charlie Murray, a successful attorney and highly decorated Vietnam veteran.

> When [Charlie's] unit president was embarrassed by a television reporter's uncovering of the appearance of error in a project, he asked Charlie who was in charge of that operation. Charlie identified one of his own direct reports.
>
> "Fire him," said the president.
>
> Charlie thought, then reflected, and then discerned, "That manager did everything I asked him to do. So I'm the one who owns the outcome. If you want to fire someone, you'd better fire me."
>
> The president paused, then changed his mind. "Never mind, Charlie," he said.
>
> Charlie's humility went so far as to allow him to immediately sacrifice his job, career, and status. He cared more for principle than for station or reward, and believes deeply in a sacrificing Lord.

I'm pretty good at accepting blame, sacrificing time, and forgoing comfort in my efforts to lead; but I catch myself flinching when I know I should sacrifice credit. People might not notice it because I deflect and give credit to my coworkers sincerely (although I do get cautious about singling out people when most good works bear the fingerprints of many). But my pride shows its head when someone else gets credit for those few things that I consider *my* achievements. If I think I'm the guy who moved the meter, I seem to want the recognition.

I don't have to waste a word convincing anyone that Jesus sacrificed due credit. His John 5 hyperbole that "the Son of Man can do nothing on his own" clearly credits the Father rather than discrediting the Son. Jesus did not take on the form of sinful flesh for the strokes. In fact, the incarnation led to just the opposite. Jesus became a man of low repute, mocked by an angry mob, a dying thief, and contemptuous soldiers.

We must be willing to sacrifice the credit we think we deserve, which most of the time should be shared and distributed anyway. As I began my tenth year as a college president I wrote a few reflections on what I had learned. One of them I entitled "The Credit Boomerang."

We must be willing to sacrifice the credit we think we deserve, which most of the time should be shared and distributed anyway.

> The first few years after my father retired from a twenty-nine-year stint overseeing a program he founded, it seemed to me he was neglected by those who carried on his work. He probably wasn't, and the sudden removal of attention didn't seem to faze him. This was the man who had so little ego that when he went to the event at which the 1974 Moody Bible Institute alumnus of the year was being announced, he whispered to my mother, "It's amazing how much this guy has in common with me."

To which she incredulously replied, "Paul, it *is* you."

I'll never forget Dad's confused expression as I looked over my mother's shoulder and realized that he was the only one of the 2,500 people present who was still in suspense.

When I entered the presidency, I followed a man who, like my father, had done his job well for thirty years; and remembering my father, I took every opportunity to tell the world what a fine job my predecessor had done. I vowed to myself that even at the risk of people bemoaning his departure, I would honor his leadership. What I discovered was the impossibility of diminishing perceptions of my effectiveness by exalting his. Credit is not a finite entity that is exhaustible when distributed. It gains energy and magnitude when freely given. Leaders need to keep themselves in a salutary frame of mind.

I have learned this credit lesson well, but my execution still needs work. My egoless father taught us repeatedly that we could accomplish much if we didn't care about receiving credit, and he was right. But I'm afraid I have taken the lesson a step too far — acting as though credit shouldn't matter to anyone. In this respect, the Golden Rule sometimes lets people like me down and should be rewritten to read, "Do unto others as they would have you do unto them." I suspect that when I fail to notice the need to give praise, it is my "ideal" self rather than my "real" self that is shrugging off the importance of credit. We all need to be appreciated for our efforts.

As I read this twelve years later, I am a little embarrassed at my delight in getting credit for giving credit. I'm sure that wasn't my only reason for discovering the circling effect of credit, but when we keep our eye on the *quid pro quo* of sacrifice, it adds bacteria to our motivation.

Hoarding credit weakens the foundation of our leadership. It is demoralizing to those who work at our sides. Giving credit empowers others. Sacrificing credit empowers us. It purifies our motives and it liberates us to work not for ourselves, but for the mission, for those who execute the mission, and for those who benefit from the mission. At the heart of our reluctance to sacrifice credit lies a dangerous territory that we have blindly staked out — what we think we deserve. Don't go there. Theologically, we're dead meat the nanosecond we bring up what we deserve. Globally, we have to argue that we have our stuff because we've earned our stuff, and everyone had a chance to get this stuff. But how do we argue that we've earned all of the accidents that plopped us into this particular lap of relative luxury? More specious arguments were never made.

Sacrifices of credit are barely sacrifices at all. They are acknowledgments, acknowledgments that we have been lavished with God's grace, that what we have "earned" compared to what we have been given takes a microscope to find.

SACRIFICING PRIVILEGE

There is a part of us that has always wanted to be like God. Satan knew what he was doing in the garden of Eden. "Pssst, Eve, would you like to be as smart as God?" "Well, yeah." But Satan didn't tell the whole story. Being like God means sacrifice upon sacrifice. Paul traces Christ's sacrifices: he made himself nothing; he took on the form of a man, and a servant at that; and he humbled himself further by accepting death, even death on a cross.

I began this chapter by contending that the sacrifices of leaders create a culture of leadership. As I mentioned in chapters 2 and 4, the most reliable leadership principle ever written is the one written on the human psyche: what you give is what you get. When a leader sacrifices for the group, the group sacrifices for the leader. In a similar way, when the leader sacrifices for the mission, the group sacrifices for the mission. If we wish to lead with Christ's incarnation as our example, our most incontestable sacrifice will be privilege.

After reading Sebastian Junger's *The Perfect Storm* while spending four days on a friend's boat, I made sure I read Alfred Lansing's *The*

Endurance, an account of Lord Ernest Shackleton's 1914–16 trip to Antarctica, peeking out from under my bed covers. I would need to trade brains with a bungee jumper to understand why a bunch of guys signed up for Hall of Fame misery and treachery in order to say they sailed to the South Pole. But they did, and not one of them would have lived to tell about it had it not been for Shackleton's leadership. He was smart and he was foolish, but most of all he was inspiring. Crew member Walter Howe told how Shackleton created a culture of equality by sacrificing the privilege to supervise. He wrote:

> Everybody more or less mucked in. It didn't matter who they were or what they were; their qualifications didn't count for anything. The doctors used to take their turn at the wheel, they'd give a hand in the galley, they'd go aloft and take in sail, and they'd set sail from the deck. Everybody was a utility firm, as it were.

He went on to say:

> Shackleton was consistently self-sacrificing. He never let his crewmen go without a comfort that he had the power to give. At one of the stops on the floes, Hurley gave someone his gloves to hold, then jumped into the *Caird* in a quick departure and forgot to retrieve them. Shackleton saw that Hurley had no gloves, took off his own, and thrust them at him. Hurley, tough and uncomplaining, refused, but Shackleton insisted and said he'd throw them overboard if he didn't take them. (Cited in Margot Morrell and Stephanie Capparell, *Shackleton's Way: Leadership Lessons from the Great Antarctic Explorer* [Penguin, 2002], p. 55)

Against the excesses of twenty-first-century captains of industry stands a ship captain who reinforced his positional authority with a metallic moral authority, forged by sacrificing many of his privileges. When leaders wait in line, bus their own tables, get their own coffee, and use the same rule book as those they have been called to lead, they do nothing to erode their respect. In fact, all the evidence suggests they enjoy greater respect than the potentates who act like they are potentates.

We sacrifice because of who we are and who God is. We sacrifice because of God's sacrifice. Our greatest treasure is not one we earned, nor one that gives us reason to boast. The apostle Paul writes:

> *But we have this treasure in jars of clay to show that this all-surpassing power is from God and not from us. We are hard pressed on every side, but not crushed; perplexed, but not in despair; persecuted, but not abandoned; struck down, but not destroyed. We always carry around in our body the death of Jesus, so that the life of Jesus may also be revealed.*
>
> **2 Corinthians 4:7 – 10**

Leadership without sacrifice is not Christian leadership. No Christian leader can claim exemption from Paul's plea: "Therefore, I urge you, brothers, in view of God's mercy, to offer your bodies as living sacrifices, holy and pleasing to God — this is your spiritual act of worship" (Romans 12:1). Sacrifice lies at the heart of God's incarnation.

Dietrich Bonhoeffer lived and died among normal people led by a brutal and power-drunken regime. Although he denounced the German people's apathy and the German church's complicity, he reserved his strongest condemnation for the Nazis. In Bonhoeffer's mind, they made power and evil almost indistinguishable. So, how could Bonhoeffer worship a God known only by his power, strength, and impregnability? In fact, he couldn't. In his *Letters from Prison* he confessed that "only a suffering God could help." In other words, it was the sacrificing God, not the omnipotent God, that sustained Bonhoeffer to his death.

I fear we have made the victorious God the only God we want to follow. Yet, the only God ever to set foot on this planet is the suffering God, the sacrificing God, the incarnate God who conquered death on the cross. If we allow the example of this God-man Jesus to influence the way we lead, I am certain people will find us in their midst, open, humble, gracious, truthful, and sacrificing. May it be so of you and me.

A FINAL THOUGHT

Thank you for reading this book. I am very honored. I don't know if you found it hard to read, but I found it hard to write. The reality of Christ's example shames much of the way I lead. You probably feel the same. We get tickled with ourselves. People look up to us and we like it. We defend our actions as adapting to our culture, "just like Jesus did." He didn't wear cheap sandals; neither should we. We're okay. Other leaders assure us that it's just fine to stay with them on the pedestals. I just opened my *Christianity Today* and on the very first page was an advertisement about a forum on "*Servant* Leadership." If I get one of the *limited* seats, I can "hear from an *elite* cross-section of renowned Christian leaders and leadership experts ... during this *exclusive event*." Exclusive, limited, elite, servant — all in the same breath. Why would the organizers of this event think making it *exclusive* will make it attractive? Because they know us so well.

It's quite possible our basic concepts of leadership run counter to God's ideal. It's quite possible that we have utterly sold out to a worldly understanding of what it means to lead. God loved David and helped him become a great king. But, according to the record in 1 Samuel 8, the very office of king was a concession God made reluctantly. The Israelite elders told Samuel that he was getting old. It was time they had a king, just like the other nations. Samuel, feeling like a failure, reported this to God. Of course, God told Samuel he wasn't the problem, it was God they were rejecting. Samuel followed God's orders and warned the Israelites to be careful what they wished for, that this would be a form of leadership they would regret. But the Israelites wouldn't budge. They still wanted a king. God said, "Okay, give them their king." Basically, God accommodated the Israelites' wishes and gave them an inferior leadership model.

Could it be that today's leadership models fall nowhere close to God's ideal? Could it be that God would prefer humble leaders like Jesus rather than today's kinglike leaders? Is there a leadership message in the story of the incarnate Christ's arrival on planet earth? Was God making a point when he gave ringside seats to smelly shepherds and a collection of barnyard animals, while the king was definitely not invited to the event?

Is there a leadership message in the story of the incarnate Christ's arrival on planet earth? Was God making a point when he gave ringside seats to smelly shepherds and a collection of barnyard animals, while the king was definitely not invited to the event?

I think it is quite possible that God works with our leadership in the same way he favored some of the Israelite kings. He blesses our best efforts to obey and glorify him through our leadership; but that blessing takes place within the context of leadership models we've taken from the world. As culture offers privilege and rank to those who lead well, followers of Christ simply accept what they're offered, and maybe there isn't really anything wrong with that. Certainly, we can lean in a Christlike direction within contemporary positions and paradigms of leadership. Many wonderful Christian leaders do just that, and I thank God for their faithful example.

But I am unsettled by the possibility that Christian concepts and models of leadership represent a modern version of Israel's desire for leadership "like the other nations." I don't think today's hierarchies and reward systems would be God's first choice. But what do we do? I don't know. I only know how I am going to respond.

First, I feel stuck, like many of you. I don't see how, in a grand sense, I can abandon the contemporary forms and structures of organizational life. I think I have to fight from within. I can't totally snub culture's attachment of privilege and pedestal to the university presidency. Also, my industry feels intractable. If I work toward the eradication of rank and tenure while moving to a fully egalitarian structure, I can't keep Whitworth in business. Neither current nor prospective faculty/staff would find our work conditions "fair." When we index fairness to an ideal rather than to the marketplace, we can't compete with reality. I do not feel free to risk the well-being of our students and employees on the chance that God has a radically different ideal and that I know what it is. But I think it is good for me to be nervous about the entire leadership system within which I am trying to lead in a way that is pleasing to God.

Second, I will live with the knowledge that these twenty-first-century forms and structures are cultural constructs, not God's forms and structures. I will look for ways to make our organization more like the body of Christ, both in climate and structure. While I may not be able to shape a university in a way that defies all of postsecondary education, I can attack all organizational characteristics that seem counter to high Christian values. It is just wrong for me to throw up my hands and accept distance and exaltation as part of the job.

In the summer of 2006 I was both encouraged and sobered by an experience with three dear friends who serve as presidents at Wake Forest University, Pepperdine University, and Trinity International University. Through the generosity of the Murdock Charitable Trust, I hosted these friends and their spouses for three days of conversation about how we go about our jobs and our lives. Toward the end of our time together, the other presidents, all of very humble self-estimations, explained how their campus cultures circumscribe their behavior in a way that would make it difficult for them to "dwell among" in the same way that I try to go about it. I was encouraged that they noticed my attempts. But I was sobered when I realized that very powerful forces keep us from acts of equality and openness. The pedestal tethers grow not only from our own enjoyment of privilege but also from well-intentioned traditions that bring predictability and order to an organizational culture. But then I was encouraged again as we all talked about ways we can change our cultures incrementally while working within them to lead in more humble, Christlike ways.

Finally, I will try and I will fail and I will try again to resemble the leadership of Jesus. My leadership tilts naturally toward me and not toward the people I lead. But I am redeemed and should not trust the impulses of my old nature. I must try to stand transparently, graciously, truthfully, and sacrificially among those I lead. I'm certain this is how Jesus calls me to lead. And I will try to live out my calling with humility, putting the mission of my organization above my own desires. Most of all, I will try to lead in a way that reflects the miracle of God's incarnation and the glory of the incarnate Christ. I invite you to join me in the effort.

QUESTIONS FOR REFLECTION AND DISCUSSION

1. Can you recall a specific example where a parent or loved one sacrificed in order to make your life better? What effect did that have on you?
2. Have there been opportunities where you felt led to sacrifice your time to help someone but decided against it? What were your reasons? What did you gain from passing up that opportunity? What did you lose?
3. In many ways, Christian leaders sacrifice every day in ways that few understand or notice. Is it fair to ask leaders to sacrifice more? Explain.
4. In what ways does the sacrifice of a leader create a culture of leadership in an organization?
5. The author states that the primary motivation for performing sacrificial acts is not the inspiration of those you lead, but the subordination of your will to the mission of your organization. In what ways does your organization's mission call you to sacrifice?